ALASTAIR C. ROSS

THE DISCIPLINE OF LOVE

THE DISCIPLINE OF LOVE
The Ten Commandments for Today

Martin Israel

First published in Great Britain 1985
SPCK
Holy Trinity Church
Marylebone Road
London NW1 4DU

British Library Cataloguing in Publication Data

Israel, Martin
The discipline of Love: the Ten Commandments for today
   1. Ten commandments
   I. Title
   222'.1606 BS1285.3

   ISBN 0–281–04174–1

Type set by J&L Composition Ltd
Printed and bound in Finland by Otava

❧ Contents

How shall a young man steer an honest course?
  By holding to thy word.
With all my heart I strive to find thee;
  let me not stray from thy commandments.
                    (Psalm 119.9–10)

The children of Israel did not find in the manna all the sweetness and strength they might have found in it; not because the manna did not contain them, but because they longed for other meat.
      (St John of the Cross, *Ascent of Mount Carmel*)

∾ Introduction

Each of the world's great religious faiths contains a body of ethical teaching which forms the foundation for the spiritual wisdom that is the glory of that tradition. The essence of this wisdom is the presence of a supreme reality that we may call God and a way of spiritual development whereby the human being may approach that reality and even attain union with it. For this purpose there are, in addition to the sacramental life, the time-honoured spiritual exercises of meditation and prayer.

At present meditation is especially widely canvassed, while the ethical foundation of the spiritual life, perhaps because it is taken for granted, is often overlooked. But in fact there can be no union with the divine until we have practised right dealing with our fellow creatures. In the Judeo-Christian tradition the Ten Commandments, or Decalogue, stand at the head of right human relationships. They were imparted by God to Moses on Mount Sinai, and are the prerequisite for the good life. Later on they were to be distilled into the principle of love. Both Jesus and his older contemporary, the Pharisee Hillel, saw that loving God with our whole being and loving our neighbour as ourself fulfilled all the Law. However, the popular concept of love has strongly individualistic overtones, being often equated merely with feelings of goodwill and affection. The discipline behind real loving is sadly lacking in this emotional response which is liable to evaporate when the object of its concern ceases to please the person.

Therefore the hard lessons of self-control embodied in the Commandments are still pertinent to the human condition. The advent of Christ has in no way challenged the validity of the moral law. On the contrary, it has underlined the Law's demands even more strongly, but by the power of love which Christ came to bestow on the created order, it has made the way of its fulfilment not only more attainable but also more joyful. There is a forbidding element in the ethical teachings of the world's religions, especially starkly articulated in the Ten Commandments, which has led to their being dismissed as essentially negative by their critics. But when the teachings are infused with the spirit of love, their strict demands become a labour of delight, an invitation to the heavenly banquet.

1 ✴ The Knowledge of God

'You shall have no other god to set against me'
(Exodus 20.3).

One bitter lesson we all have to learn is our failure day by day to
live the high ideals we set before ourselves. St Paul diagnosed this
tragic flaw in human nature precisely when he wrote:

> We know that the law is spiritual; but I am not: I am unspiritual,
> the purchased slave of sin. I do not even acknowledge my own
> actions as mine, for what I do is not what I want to do, but what I
> detest. But if what I do is against my will, it means that I agree
> with the law and hold it to be admirable. But as things are, it is no
> longer I that perform the action, but sin that lodges in me. For I
> know that nothing good lodges in me – in my unspiritual nature, I
> mean – for though the will to do good is there, the deed is not.
> The good which I want to do, I fail to do; but what I do is the
> wrong which is against my will.

He goes on to discover the principle that when he wants to do the
right only the wrong is within his reach. In his inmost self he
delights in the law of God, but in his bodily members there is
another law, fighting against the law that his reason approves and
making him a prisoner under the law that is in his members, the
law of sin (Romans 7.14–23).

To many people, especially in the currently permissive society
of the West, St Paul's agonizings are tedious, if not frankly
morbid. To enjoy oneself sensually in the flow of each moment
seems to be the most desirable end of existence – but what is this
end? Reflection shows the inevitable advance of ageing, disease
and death. If this is the height of human endeavour, man takes
his place merely as the most gifted of a vast assembly of animals,
but with no vision measurably higher than theirs.

Throughout recorded history, however, there has been a cloud
of spiritual witnesses who have lifted the veil of materialistic

delusion from the faces of their fellows to point to a destiny that transcends this fleeting mortal life and finds its summation in a fulfilment of shared existence in eternity. I believe there is a centre of awareness in all rational creatures that knows dimly, yet incontrovertibly, of a higher goal that embraces meaning and community, whose code name is God. In St Augustine's immortal words, 'You have made us for yourself alone, O God, and our hearts are restless until they rest in you'. In the end the agonized self-confrontation articulated by St Paul cannot be dismissed from our thoughts, no matter how fulfilled and emancipated we may consider ourselves. What are we, and what are we to become? This question lies at the root of all human existence, both individual and communal.

The basic requirements for civilized living are respect for our fellow creatures and a dedication of ourselves to the common good. When we give of ourselves in unstinted integrity to the community, it prospers by our contribution and in turn affords us its support and blessing. On the other hand, the mark of uncivilized behaviour is an exaltation of the self above the interests of the community. In this way we deal dishonestly with others, eventually injuring them, so that we may prosper at their expense. But this prosperity is won at a great price: the communal goodwill on which we all ultimately depend is gradually eroded until we find ourselves much disliked and isolated. This isolation from the common concern is not merely material, it also has psychic undertones. And as we cut ourselves off from human solidarity, so we find ourselves disconcertingly separated from a more subtle, pervasive source of life. This is the power of God, his Holy Spirit, on whom all life depends, from whom all life proceeds. If we are to survive, we have to acknowledge the supremacy of civilized values, ruefully perhaps, but also categorically.

But if we determine to live in a socially acceptable manner in order to gain the benefits inherent in community, we will soon slip into a way of calculated egoism that may prove as unsatisfactory as a course of frankly anti-social behaviour. Everything we do will have a price attached to it: we will expect due recompense for our communal concern, and be aggrieved if this is not forthcoming. We will tend to judge others according to our own standards, and be displeased when those less admirable than we believe ourselves seem to prosper at least as well as we do. Two possible unworthy attitudes can easily follow from this consideration: one is a puritanical separation of ourselves from all that is unclean, so that we begin to constitute a righteous elect, and the other is an insidious descent from the pinnacles of our newly-acquired morality so that we too begin to serve two standards. The one standard is what our minds approve and the other the requirements of the present moment, so that we may practise petty dishonesty when we believe we are unobserved, under the pretext that everyone else does it whenever possible and that taxation and other economic afflictions always attack our particular social class especially unfairly. In this way we slip unobtrusively into the state of divided moral consciousness that St Paul described with such topical insight. The drama of human life is the conflict between the will of the ego that strives for immediate survival in a seldom very easy environment, and the will of a higher power residing in us, around us and above us. This is the source of meaning in a larger frame of reference that embraces the individual, the community and the whole scheme of cosmic reality. In the end both wills have to coincide, for the one is incomplete without the other. If there is indeed a higher meaning to life in our incomprehensible universe, it must involve all individual creatures, and especially the human being in our little world. This is because the human mind and spirit out-distance any other sentient power on earth, and are to direct all other forms of life towards their final completion in God.

It becomes increasingly evident as we learn more about ourselves in the chequered course of our lives, that of ourselves we can do little that is good. Occasionally we may attain near-perfection, as when we are punctual for an appointment or perform a task exactly according to its specification, but we fall from this high standard in due course. Likewise, our relationships with others, so cordial and open in love on one occasion, soon falter in insensitivity, unawareness and frank indifference. Some of us may have experienced peaks of intimate knowledge about the nature of reality, but soon the shadow of worldly desire falls and we find ourselves shrouded in a mist of darkness and inquietude. In those peaks of near-perfection we are especially close to God by his grace and through our unwonted openness. But this grace cannot be bargained for, let alone taken for granted. What we have been shown in a moment of illumination has now to be bought to become our own. The price is far beyond money; nothing less than our own being can suffice. We begin to discern the first truth of life, that only in the power of God can we fulfil the requirements of civilized life constantly, joyfully, and above all communally. Therefore the first great

3

commandment is to worship God alone, because until he is with us as a conscious presence, all our other endeavours will fail in practice and remain mere ideals of wishful thought.

But how do we know God? He cannot be conjured up, delineated or compared with any sensual or conceptual image. As soon as we try to describe God we simply describe our own view of life or our image of perfection. If we could limit or define God's presence we would bring God down to our level and start worshipping our own mind, or even a construct of that mind. Of God nothing can be said, and yet he is the source of all knowledge. He is the secret force from whom all creation flows, yet he cannot be known with the mind. But once he is known, he informs the mind, which then becomes increasingly aware of his presence. Until we have become like him, we can approach him rationally only in terms of paradox. He is so unlike anything we know with the senses that he can be spoken of only in negative terms, of what he is not. And as we move into the 'apophatic' theology of complete negation, so we become more transparent ourselves, and the solid ego gives way to a centre of luminous peace within us where God can be known. As the writer of *The Cloud of Unknowing* says, 'By love may he be gotten and holden, but by thought never'.

Yet love itself cannot be contrived; it comes from God, being indeed the essential energy of God to his creatures. The knowledge of God's love is the basis of our love to him and to our fellow creatures: we love because he loved us first (1 John 4.19). It follows therefore that the essential, indeed surpreme, human action is a willed openness to the present moment. It is a right mindfulness in which we are empty of conceit, all previously held views, and all certitude so that we can take in the glory of the moment in hand, where time intersects with eternity. In the words of the Magnificat, 'The hungry he has satisfied with good things, the rich sent empty away' (Luke 1.53). The rich are sent away empty of the one thing necessary for life because they are crammed with inessential dross, whereas the hungry are empty of self-importance, being eager only for the knowledge of God's presence. It not infrequently transpires that this hunger follows a course of disaster when the inessentials are forcibly stripped from us and we are left so bereft that God can at last make his presence known to us. But fortunately this cataclysmic course to a knowledge of God is not inevitable: if we could but practise the awareness of the present moment, we would also be practising the presence of God, to quote the title of Brother Lawrence's famous book. 'If you search with all your heart, I will let you find me, says the Lord' (Jeremiah 29.13). This searching with the whole heart means a total self-giving to the moment in hand and to all the people who have their existence in that moment.

In order to attain this single-pointed vision at all times, the practice of contemplation is necessary both as a preliminary exercise and as a constant accompaniment in whatever situation we may find ourselves. Once we know God in silent communion he will be with us no matter where we find ourselves: he is always everywhere but until he is with us as a conscious presence, we will never know where we are or what we should be doing. Even though we may be involved in frantic activity, we will not be in command of ourselves or in control of our life. The experience is not unlike that of a sleep-walker on the path of life. Once, however, the practice of God's presence is the central action of our life, we discover that we can cope with whatever situation confronts us, for resources previously dormant in us are now awakened and can be called upon. In one-pointed vision, the gates of eternity open up for us as do the minds of our fellow creatures in this world.

The way of contemplation is one in which we give our total being, soul and body, to God and listen inwardly to what his Spirit tells us. In order to attain that absolute dedication, the mind should first be filled with good things, things provided by God himself for our welfare. This is where God's word, the great scriptures of the world, and especially the Bible, play such an important part in bringing us to him. The pious Jew has found that meditating upon the Law is an excellent way of focusing his mind upon God himself; Psalm 119, the longest of all the psalms, is a monument of meditation on the divine revelation, almost every verse of which mentions God's law of life, growth and fulfilment. St Paul's exhortation that we should fill our minds with all that is true, noble, just and pure, all that is lovable and gracious, excellent and admirable (Philippians 4.8) is especially apposite to a knowledge of God in the heart. As our thoughts are occupied with good things, so we enter a state of silence in which we approach the source of all that is good, God himself. And then we can be open to him who is always there, even when we are far away in thoughtless frivolity. At this stage the works, words and energies of God merge into a living void of silence. In that silence deep speaks to deep in the mighty roar of God's cataracts, a tumultuous silence in which the voice of God is heard by the inner ear of the soul, while the loving warmth of his embrace renews and transfigures the whole person.

5

To know effectively is to establish direct union with the other person. In the Scriptures, husband and wife know each other in tenderest sexual union before a child of promise is conceived. This knowledge can be attained only when the self is yielded in love to the other person, who in turn gives of himself to the beloved. In this mutual self-surrender God the Holy Spirit makes himself known. He so transmutes the consciousness of those who take part in the renunciation of self that they can know God directly in that same union. As we give of ourselves in selfless service and sacrificial concern, so we know God and can sustain that relationship as long as we remain in an attitude of humble self-giving to the other.

'How blest are those whose hearts are pure; they shall see God' (Matthew 5.8). In this beatitude Jesus sums up in a single phrase the requirement for knowing God: a heart that is empty of guile and single in dedication to the one thing needful for abundant life – the service of God. A pure heart is unsullied by selfishness; it is chaste and obedient to its highest calling. When God reveals himself to the ardent soul, he fills that person with a warmth of caring that far transcends human concern at its most passionate. It is in this experience of union with God that we can use the personal pronoun to describe the divine relationship with the creature. It may be argued that the masculine image evoked by the pronoun 'he' ignores the tender, feminine aspect of God's love, but, on the other hand, it does emphasize its executive power. In the end, all words fail to do justice to God's presence, and we can grasp ineffectively only at what is given us. Whenever we say that God is love we are affirming our acceptance of a personal God. This is because love can never ignore the individual, no matter how small and insignificant it may appear to others. All were created by God, the noxious no less than the serviceable, and their resurrection is part of the mystery of life itself. As we enter into the divine darkness where God shows himself to the naked soul, so these rationally impenetrable mysteries become acceptable, almost logical, in a broader frame of reference. The mind of God can alone penetrate the suffering of the created universe to see the glorious unfolding of the divine will for all his creatures. As we enter this realm of light in contemplative prayer, so God's grace inflames our soul with renewed love and heightened understanding, and we too can begin to see eternal truth.

Once we know God in the fellowship of silent dedication, we come to be filled with his Spirit and to resemble his Son, in

THE KNOWLEDGE OF GOD

whom humanity and divinity reside in perfect union. 'And because for us there is no veil over the face, we all reflect as in a mirror the splendour of the Lord; thus we are transfigured into his likeness from splendour to splendour. Such is the influence of the Lord who is Spirit' (2 Corinthians 3.18). Indeed, in this unobstructed vision, 'God is light, and in him there is no darkness at all' (1 John 1.5). As we contemplate that light, so the darkness that is in us and in the world around us is outlined, accentuated and concentrated. But as it is confronted in the light of God's love, it is cleared and transfigured. In this experience of the healing power of God's uncreated light we believe that all that is unhealed will finally be brought close to the divine presence in supreme radiance.

To acknowledge God as the source of all that is loving, truthful and beautiful – the platonic triad of virtues that leads the rational mind through the soul to God – is to put him above all else in one's estimation. It means consecrating oneself to live the life of love, truth and beauty, and filling the world around one with the radiance of that beauty. With God in one's heart and understanding, this supreme human endeavour at last becomes more than a counsel of perfection; it can take off from the ground and become a living venture. And the wonder of it all is this: God can be approached at will by the simple exercise of clearing one's mind of all thoughts, asking a burning question, and waiting in rapt attention for the answer, as if about to hear a world-shattering pronouncement. In the silent waiting, in the awe of the present moment, God is eternally known. In the suspense of that moment the mind is empty of all guile and full of dedication in anticipation of meeting the truth. In its stillness it receives the still small voice of God himself. Prayer itself is in essence a waiting on God. Indeed, in the life of an aspiring person all conversation with God is progressively transfigured into luminous silence in which the divine will is manifest. We learn that we do not have to ask God for things so much as to offer ourselves to him in service, so that through us the whole world may be filled with those things. This in turn can come about only as the consciousness of all people is raised above selfish demands for comfort to a peak of self-giving service for their neighbours. Then alone will we cease to do evil and learn to do good. Then alone will the divided consciousness that St Paul described so poignantly be healed and mankind live as an integrated whole in constructive unity with all living forms.

For this visionary state of self-transcendence to be attained, let it be said at once that there must be social justice. The individual's demands for comfort are not in themselves to be derided, let alone decried. Until all people have the means to live in health and dignity, there can be no spiritual advance for the world as a whole. It is when personal comfort takes precedence over all other considerations that it becomes destructive, because it assumes a selfish, ultimately predatory insistence, battening on other people and on all life. In this lies the strength of Jesus' command, 'Set your mind on God's kingdom and his justice before everything else, and all the rest will come to you as well' (Matthew 6.33). The explanation of this spiritual law is that when the mind is set in confidence and dedication on God's Kingdom and his law, his Holy Spirit infuses us with special strength and we are enabled to do things that would previously have been beyond our capability. When our own ego is the determining guide to action we become anxious, neurotically obsessive, emotionally unstable and increasingly despotic in our relationships. The more we strain, the less we gain. But when we are open to God, inner resources become unblocked, and we are amazed at our own strength. At last we need strive no longer only for our own well-being, but can give of ourselves in concern for our neighbour also. In this way rivalry and competition can gradually yield to co-operation and solidarity with others without there being any slackening of activity or dulling of ideals of perfection. To serve becomes life's supreme joy; to work in harmony with one's peers becomes a constant source of happiness.

When the experience of God's love permeates our very being, we begin to see clearly for the first time in our lives. For it is then that the Holy Spirit renews our body, illuminates our mind, purifies our emotional life and ennobles our soul, which is the seat of moral decisions and the point where our true self is revealed. The experience of God shows us who we really are and sets us free to be ourselves and become what we were destined to be – sons of God in the image of the eternal Word, which Christians see enshrined in the person of Christ. When we can respond rationally to that image, we begin to see how privileged we are to be born human. Then we realize how unacceptable we are until we give ourselves, body and soul, to the service of the world and the healing of all that is in pain. Such are the thoughts that God's presence inspires in our minds; such is the impetus to the will that follows from these considerations. Only as we return to God with many others in our care will we fulfil the high destiny of mortal life.

True religion brings the human personality to the threshold of immense splendour. It reveals the futility of a life that evades the burning issues of meaning and destiny. These existential questions of life can never be fully answered by the reasoning mind, but as we enter the divine grace, so new insights are vouchsafed us. As we partake of them, so we actualize a little of the divinity latent in us also, for we are all potential Christs. Once the vision has been opened to us, we may never turn our backs on it, for then we will have committed the sin against the Holy Spirit, and life itself will recede from our grasp. It is indeed a terrible thing to fall into the hands of the living God (Hebrews 10.31), for now the absolute demand is made on us: become fully human, as Jesus was human. But if we evade this challenge, we remain self-absorbed animals, whom the earth will in due course swallow up as it did Korah and his followers (Numbers 16.31–3). It is at this juncture that God's love and justice come together, and we see that he controls the darkness, even though he is visible as uncreated light. In that dual dominion of God lies our mortal hope.

2 ❧ Purity of Worship

'You shall not make a carved image for yourself nor the likeness of anything in the heavens above, or on the earth below, or in the waters under the earth. You shall not bow down to them or worship them' (Exodus 20.4–5).

When we worship something we attribute supreme worth to it, so that we offer our very lives for it. In our scale of values it assumes the dominant, indeed final, place and to it all our efforts and endeavours are directed. Such an object, be it inanimate or living, rapidly assumes the quality of a god, and we sacrifice ourselves to attain the power, security or invulnerability that its possession promises. But, in the end, it limits us to its own finitude so that we become imprisoned in its form and cannot attain that freedom to be a son of God which is our natural destiny. The primitive urge towards worship of cultic objects is related to our human insecurity. The mystery of creation fills the ignorant person with a special reverence for certain places and natural phenomena that appear to be in contact with supernatural forces. These, if placated, will bestow good fortune on the votary, but if neglected may cast a shadow of failure on all he attempts, eventually destroying him and his family. Superstition is an irrational fear of the unknown or unexplained elements of life which are blindly but doggedly placated by the obsessional sacrifice of a person's time and substance. It was in this spirit that our forebears bowed down before objects of wood, stone or metal as images of the Deity. They were idols, and idolatry, though much subtler in our present incomparably more sophisticated world, remains the great deceiver in our quest after wholeness.

'For where your treasure is, there will your heart be also' (Matthew 6.20). Anything less than God himself fails to fulfil the human potential, for in him alone do we find the peace of perfect fellowship with all creation.

The things of this world that effectively usurp the role of the Deity in the lives of many people include such obvious idols as wealth and mundane possessions. The more we have, the more secure do we feel until the moment of truth dawns when all is removed from us and we have only the naked soul to call our own. In the story of the rich man who had so much that he decided to collect all his wealth in storehouses and then to relax and have a good time for the remainder of his life (Luke 12.17–21), Jesus warns us that at any moment that same man may be called on to surrender all he has amassed, and then he will appear naked of all worth before God; our very life is in God's power, and all we have accumulated here is an illusion if it serves merely to enhance our identity. Possessions afford us no security if we are not secure within ourselves; once we know God within we can share all we possess with those outside. Then only do money and material goods attain value as part of God's providence to human beings while they are living in this world.

Another idol we worship is human intimacy, which then removes us from a broader commitment to mankind generally. A parent, child or spouse can be the central focus of a person's identity, the point around which his whole life revolves. When this relationship is severed, whether by death or controversy, the core of meaning fades from that person's life. He ceases to function as an independent being, so that he may quit life's race on a suicidal note. The value of deep human relationships is that they teach us basic lessons in loyalty, forbearance and sacrifice; the family is the unit of civilized life. But there comes a time when even the closest-knit group must fall asunder like the petals of an ageing flower. Death sets its seal on all possessions, and unless we have learned to bestow our caring on a wider community, we will remain bereft. Of this we shall have more to say when we consider our parental relationship in terms of God's commandment to us. Human relationships flourish best in the spirit of service; they wilt when possessiveness takes root. Their end is a growing empathy with all life.

Another insidious idol that frequently dominates our life is the opinion of other people; what they think about us – or, to be more accurate, what we believe they think about us – sometimes becomes the overriding focus of our concern. To a certain extent this aberration finds its source in the powerful figures that directed our lives when we were small, our parents and teachers. Conditioning is the basis of coming to learn the manners and customs of the society into which we were born and with which we are to live and assert ourselves. By the approval we earn or the hostility we evoke, we learn to temper our actions and attitudes to the current social climate. This tendency to trim one's sails to the prevailing wind allows one to adapt oneself to those around one, and live in a socially acceptable way. But there is also a spark of God in all of us that will not rest until we have actualized our own gifts and established our unique identity in the society around us. The balance between self-actualization on the one hand and obedience to the common good on the other is a fine one, and depending on our synthesis of these potentially conflicting tendencies lies our ultimate contribution to life. In fact real self-actualization is in the common interest, for then we give of our best to the community.

The Freudian super-ego includes a constellation of master figures from our youth that continue to exert a psychic stranglehold on our development as an individual in our own right. This complex can attach itself later on in life to any special person whom we admire or whose support we covet. In the end our behaviour can be modified, even deflected, by this powerful, unconscious focus in our midst. Quite often the insecurity within lies concealed behind the outer image we contrive. What effect we make on other people becomes the foundation of our shaky identity. In this way our reputation becomes our god, and anything that may happen to impugn it our greatest dread. Likewise, those younger and more gifted than ourselves become our greatest threat, and we begin to demean them subtly so that they may be discredited by others. The reputation we have acquired is our way of relating to the super-ego figure within as well as our peers in the world outside.

It is probable that our reputation is our dearest idol: to accuse a person of meanness or humourlessness is to offer him an insult that he will not lightly tolerate. In the sufferings of Job it was, in all probability, the evaporation of his previous reputation for philanthropy and wisdom that hurt him most deeply. We can adapt ourselves to outer loss more easily than to inner humiliation; this, too, was Christ's final pain, reviled by the populace as he hung crucified between two criminals. By his suffering all suffering is ennobled and all personal darkness illuminated by the love he shared with those in pain. Only when the idols of popular esteem and personal reputation have been expunged – in fact they are reverse sides of the same coin – can we know ourselves naked in the presence of the true God who accepts us for what we are, and not merely for what we tried to achieve in the strange world we inhabit. Achievement that lasts lifts up the world closer to God; all else is illusion.

In his *Tales of the Hasidim – Later Masters*, Martin Buber recounts the teaching of Rabbi Bunam of Pzhysha, who was once asked what was meant by the expression 'sacrificing to idols': surely no one would really bring a sacrifice to an idol? The rabbi replied by giving an example of a devout, righteous man, sitting at table with others. He would like to eat a little more but refrains because of what people might think of him: this is sacrificing to idols. In this example it is the mental attitude that determines the idolatry of the action: had the good man refrained lest he lead the common folk into gluttony, his renunciation would have been commendable. St Paul makes a somewhat related point in relation to food consecrated to heathen deities in 1 Corinthians 8, when he says that if food be the downfall of one's brother, one should no longer eat meat. While the enlightened man is aware of the non-existence of false gods, the ignorant attributes power to a consecration of food in their name, and the weak conscience is polluted by the eating.

From all this we can see that idolatry is often close to true sanctity in outer form, but that its inner motive is corrupt; it exalts the creature above the Creator. It also exalts the ego above the true self that lies enshrined in the soul and whose cardinal function is to judge values. The ego looks for immediate recognition whereas the true self is satisfied only with the vision of God, in whose image it was created. If we set our sights to anything less than – or other than – that supreme attainment, we fail to realize our full potential, and thereby betray our high calling to be sons of God in the likeness of the Son, Jesus Christ. This is the essence of sin, to fail to reach the mark set for us in our own person. When God is the centre of our lives, that mark is never far from our gaze, and even if through human weakness we are deflected intermittently from it, the light of God will soon draw us back again. And God's nature is always to forgive the person who is penitent.

But our image of God can itself become an insidious idol. This is where religion can be a dangerous snare no less than a divine blessing. At its best a religious tradition, with its established forms of worship, its sacraments and its communal concern, is a way of leading the aspiring person past egoistical preoccupation to a commitment to all life in God. Indeed, the closer we are to God, the more nearly do all the great religious traditions of the world come together; their saints and mystics speak a common language as sectarian religion yields to the divine vision. In the New Jerusalem there is no temple, for the sovereign Lord God and the Lamb are its temple (Revelation 21.22): religion has expanded into a universal spirituality, in which the Holy Spirit infuses all creation with new life. But religion, if it becomes arrogant and triumphalistic, can usurp the place of God in the lives of the multitude. It becomes a supernatural type of insurance against worldly ills, and all misfortunes are attributed to subversion against its authority. A theocracy is often the most terrible form of despotism: all who threaten the interests of the sectarian functionaries can be summarily condemned and executed as enemies of God. Religious intolerance assumes the cruellest perversions, because the fanatic's very life depends on his certainty of possessing the entire truth. A true religion leads the follower to an encounter with God, whose presence infuses him with the fruits of the Holy Spirit, especially love, joy and peace. A false religion leads to an encounter with the demonic which masquerades as the Deity, but which ends in imbalance, fanaticism and total disintegration of the personality. Furthermore, all the great religious traditions of the world have their unbalanced fringe, where illusion and deception cloud the vision of God.

Our very attempt to describe God in human terms brings with it a subtle idolatry. The God of the early Old Testament, for instance, is a vengeful deity, described in the second commandment, which we are now considering, as jealous. He punishes the children for the sins of the fathers to the third and fourth generations of those who hate him, but keeps faith with thousands, with those who love him and keep his commandments (Exodus 20.5–6). That those who contravene the law of God ultimately suffer is a fact of life, but the image of a dictatorial, cruel potentate is not one that can lead us either to freedom or to the abundant life. Our reaction to such a being can hardly avoid the extremes of obsessional fear, lest we displease him, and obsequious obedience, in order to placate him. His followers may be kept on a straight path of morality, but only at the expense of their inner integrity, and there is little possibility of spiritual growth. Such an idol of God, an anthropomorphic being of power and jealousy, has harried the lives of many devout religionists, often precipitating obsessional neurotic breakdowns and generally casting an ominous shadow of gloom and foreboding. They go about in constant fear that they have inadvertently offended this image, perhaps by committing the terrible sin against the Holy Spirit.

As the spiritual consciousness of the Jews matured, so God was perceived in more positive terms – as a father having compassion on his children. Indeed, the radiant Psalm 103 is one paean of praise to the God of love – compassionate and gracious, long-suffering and forever constant – later to be revealed in the life of Jesus, who is appropriately seen as the human face of God. But even this approach to God as personal warmth can be inadequate. There is a mystery to life that transcends all our concepts, and the more we have experienced, the less do we speak of God, except in terms of awe. Yet it is an awe attached to a personal presence, whom we know more imtimately than our closest friend. Love seeks the fulfilment of the person to his highest, and therefore predestined, potential. It is chaste and discriminating as well as warm and welcoming. God is indeed jealous, not for his reputation but for us. As a loving parent is jealous for the reputation of his children, so is God the Father jealous for the integrity of his creatures. In this respect wrath is wounded love: all that prevents us fulfilling our high calling as sons of God contravenes the divine law of love. We will continue to suffer until we turn again and fulfil the purpose of our lives, a purpose known to God in eternity and to us in the depth of the soul. In other words, the love of God is not a sentimental effusion; it is a ceaseless outpouring of himself for the life of his creatures. In this divine self-giving there is a humorous unpredictability, reminding us that the Holy Spirit blows where he likes and is not directed by the human will. God refuses to give Moses a finite name for himself: he is what he is, and as we become what we are to become, so we will know him ever more intimately. He is within us, above us, and, in Christ, alongside us also in life's precarious journey. We know him best when we cease to think about him, but get on with living and serving others. In self-forgetful service to the world we are especially close to God. It is then that his influence is most evident to us, for the Holy Spirit is guiding us in our individual work of healing and redemption.

Since the knowledge of God is not directly available to the reasoning faculty and transcends all created things, it is easy to fall into the error of disparaging the creation and despising rational thought. Our quest for God is, on the other hand, through the created world and the faculties of the personality with which we have been endowed. If a person cannot perceive the divine presence in the world around him, he is unlikely to sense it in any other dimension. While the creation must never be confused with the Creator, it is nevertheless true that God leaves traces of his activity in every phenomenon we experience. As Psalm 19 reminds us, the heavens tell out the glory of God, the vault of heaven reveals his handiwork. In the words of Psalm 24, the earth is the Lord's and all that is in it, the world and those who dwell therein. Psalm 104 is a triumphant rhapsody on the natural world of God's creation, a theme enlarged on in God's great manifestation of himself to Job. The creation in all its forms leads us to worship the Creator, in whose presence the world itself is transformed in splendour. All created life has a sacramental significance – it is an outer and visible sign of an inner and spiritual grace. It is to be lifted up from the bondage of mortality and decay to enter into the eternal glory of God by human consecration. Man is God's priest in our little world, and when he acts according to the law of love and service, he hastens the day of universal redemption and resurrection.

Therefore, when we consider our ancestors who bowed down before carved images, we can see that it was in their action in reducing the Deity to a finite form that their error lay. Once, however, we know God in the height of contemplation and the depth of shared suffering with those around us, we can appreciate and rejoice in the wonderful things of this world. The mystics have always felt intuitively that a cosmic empathy pervades and unites all things. The stoic Marcus Aurelius said, 'All things are intertwined; there is practically nothing alien from other things, since all things have been set in order and make up the one cosmos. For there is one cosmos and one God through all, and one substance and one law and one common reason and one truth'. St Paul in addressing the Athenians used this approach when he spoke of God as not being far from each one of us, for in him we live and move and in him we exist (Acts 17.28). As W. R. Inge writes in *Mysticism in Religion*, 'The conviction that there is a unity underlying all diversity is an article of faith with all mystics; it is an ultimate truth which in our imperfect state must be apprehended by faith, not by sight. Panpsychism becomes dangerous and even absurd if we hold that the Deity is equally manifested in all phenomena.' It is here that our scale of values is of cardinal importance. Bread and wine, articles of our common diet, easily degenerate into means of gluttony and debauchery; however, when consecrated, they become the very Body and Blood of Christ, by whom all things were made. He gives of himself perpetually for the redemption of the world from the bondage of sin to enter into the glory of the risen life.

All matter is potentially holy because God made it, used it in the Incarnation of Christ, and renews it constantly by his Holy Spirit. We humans have the power to use it for our own purposes, but unless we are inspired by God, we will defile it and destroy its beauty. Once we have repented of our selfish disregard for nature and dedicate ourselves anew and without reserve to the service of God and our fellow creatures, matter receives the blessing of God transmitted by the human touch. Then we cease to do evil and start to do good. The same principle holds true for religious worship. The very beauty of music and the nobility of architecture can interpose human skill and power between the humble worshipper and God, when the professional participants are full of their own magnificence and forgetful of the One from whom all glory arises. Some church services assume the character of sacred concerts, just as others seem to exist primarily to display the gifts of the preacher. They entertain and even edify, but they do not bring the congregation close to God, whom the sensitive will feel to be nearer to them in the solitude of their own abode or in the tranquil beauty of nature. On the other hand, if the lives of those who participate in the act of worship are dedicated wholeheartedly to God, the decor and music are sacrifices of the human spirit to him, and all who are met together in prayer are lifted up consciously to heaven, where divine radiance and human transparency come together. This is an even greater tribute to God's providence than solitary worship, because it embraces corporate solidarity.

Let us therefore thank God for the manifold gifts he has bestowed on us: the radiance of a healthy body, the exaltation of an aspiring mind, the warmth of an emotional life fulfilled in the fellowship of those whom we love, and the illumination of a soul infused by the Holy Spirit. Man inhabits the earth, but his ultimate abode is in the eternal realm in union with God. He is to bring the world with him, transfigured and resurrected, as the mortal body of Jesus was raised up in spiritual splendour after the crucifixion. In this context we can thank God for our possessions and wealth, remembering that we are merely stewards and not owners. We can exult in our intellectual and artistic gifts, rejoicing in the happiness and freedom they afford others on whom we bestow them without reserve. Our reputation itself becomes a bulwark of integrity to others with whom we can share our own knowledge, while those we love cease to be mere emotional supports but become the way of a greater dedication of ourselves to many different types of people whom previously we would have disregarded. As Jesus says in the parable of the talents, 'The man who has will always be given more, till he has enough and to spare; and the man who has not will forfeit even what he has' (Matthew 25.29).

The material world is our place of experience and growth, of experimentation and sacrifice. We use its substance in the many varied activities of our life, at first with the thoughtless abandon of youth and later with the more sober responsibility of increasing age. In our turn we are to glorify all that we touch, so that compliant matter may be blessed by our usage. The sacraments of the Church remind us of the holiness inherent in such common articles of everyday usage as bread, wine, water and oil. When we live the life of awareness of the divine presence in each moment, we begin to impart holiness to whatever we handle and to whomsoever we meet. A blessing flows out from us to the world, and the day of general resurrection draws closer.

Thus, although nothing that is visible or tangible can be worshipped as an image of God, when we are close to God, we can see the holiness of all that he has fashioned. We can thank him for it and, in his presence, play our part in its transfiguration.

3 ✎ The Holiness of God

**'You shall not make wrong use of the name of the Lord
your God; the Lord will not leave unpunished the man
who misuses his name'** (Exodus 20.7).

The Lord is beyond all names, but it is all too easy to attain a
familiarity with the Deity as a person through thoughtless usage
in daily life. This can be nourished by formal worship in which
the liturgy subtly replaces the mystery of God instead of leading
the worshipper in awe to that mystery. An easy familiarity with
God brings with it a constant temptation to enlist his help for our
private ends. Indeed, popular religion thrives on a system of
punishments and rewards depending on our obedience to the god
image we have constructed – or, more accurately, that has been
constructed for us by our ancestors – in our own minds. It is on
this account, among others, that God cannot be adequately
spoken of in purely personal terms, no matter how positive and
edifying these may be. Embracing all personal concepts, there is
a mystery that transcends human reason. What we can name and
define we can master; what lies beyond our rational grasp can
alone lead us on to our final destination and show us what we
might become. The supreme I–Thou relationship is between
God and man, for divine knowledge is attained by perfect self-
giving; we give our naked impotence, as the publican in Jesus'
famous parable (Luke 18.9–14), and God gives his whole being,
as is his nature. In this way we are filled with the divine grace and
in time can offer ourselves without reserve to do the apportioned
work of serving the world.

Once, however, God becomes an object or a finite being that
can be manipulated by the mind, the deep transforming relationship is forfeited, and an I–It relationship of usage and convenience
takes its place. Then we begin to use God for our own ends, even
swearing falsely in his name. Perjury is indeed the ultimate evil of
this type, for here the divine name is used deliberately in attest-
ing to falsehood sworn as truth. In this way God's name can be
used to injure an innocent person. The unpremeditated use of the

divine name, sometimes in an attitude of exasperation or frivolity, or when we are agreeably surprised or deeply shocked, is far less reprehensible in that it is articulated without malice, but it trivializes what is in essence holy. To say 'Thank God' may be an exclamation of reverent gratitude for a favour received. On the other hand, it may be an ironical response to what we regard as small measure for the efforts we have made – 'Thank God for small mercies'. It is evident that the use of God's name without reverence is unnecessary and often deeply offensive. Therefore the use of the holy name should be premeditated and the pledge of a holier way of life. Indeed, the name is so holy that it should be left unuttered except in the context of prayer. When we make wrong use of the name, God is not diminished, for his holiness is inviolate. What is sullied is the divine image implanted in the depth of the soul. We are committing a grave sin inasmuch as we have betrayed something sacred in our own nature. We have failed lamentably to attain the mark set for us; indeed, we have demeaned and lowered the high calling of that mark so that it is contaminated with the stain of the world's commerce rather than illuminated by the divine effulgence. If we persist in abusing the divine name, God ceases to be a presence in our lives, and we remain rooted to a purely animal level of existence.

God's name is holy. It is sacred, and it brings sanctity to all who use it in humble reverence. The supreme prophet of God's transcendent holiness is Isaiah. His marvellous vision in the temple at the beginning of his ministry is one of the Lord lifted up above all creation so that even the angels cannot confront him directly.

> I saw the Lord seated on a throne, high and exalted, and the skirt of his robe filled the temple. About him were attendant seraphim, and each had six wings; one pair covered his face and one pair his feet, and one pair was spread in flight. They were calling ceaselessly to one another, 'Holy, holy, holy is the Lord of Hosts; the whole earth is full of his glory'. And, as each one called, the threshold shook to its foundations while the house was filled with smoke (Isaiah 6.1–4).

Isaiah was overwhelmingly conscious of his own sinfulness and the uncleanness of his compatriots as he witnessed the vision of God's holiness. Only when a seraph took a glowing coal from the heavenly altar and touched Isaiah's lips with it was his iniquity removed. Then he was ready for his prophetic mission.

St John was inspired when he wrote that God is love, a love disclosed definitively for us by his sending his only Son into the world to bring us life (1 John 4.9). But this love is something greater than our limited human understanding can encompass. God is also holiness: while love brings us together, holiness separates us from God. God is transcendent not merely of his creation, but also of the emotional life of his sentient creatures, of which the human is the most advanced in our world. They are unclean, selfish, predatory and destructive whereas he is seen as uncreated light, a fire devouring all that is unwholesome and impure. It is no wonder that the Bible repeatedly asserts that no person can see God and live. Even the great theophanies in Scripture, such as Isaiah's vision in the temple and Moses' meeting with God in the burning bush, are manifestations of the divine creative energies rather than a direct meeting with God. Likewise, in the height of union, the mystic is brought with all creation into the divine presence, whose emanation is light and whose nature is love. Yet although the divine presence is everywhere, God cannot be limited to any point or time. Furthermore, all such encounters and visions are evanescent, lasting at the most a few minutes. They give intimations to the prophet or mystic (the two are often combined functions) about the nature of eternal life, but the remainder of his earthly life has to be dedicated to bringing down to earth what he has been shown.

And yet love and holiness are not mutually exclusive; they are, on the contrary, reverse sides of the single coin of God's eternal presence and his caring for all he has created. His transcendent holiness, while inevitably separating us in our present imperfect form from him, is ultimately to purify us in the fire of life's further experience, so that we too may be holy. When the Lord spoke to Moses, he said, 'Speak to all the community of the Israelites in these words: you shall be holy because I, the Lord your God, am holy' (Leviticus 19.1–2). The Decalogue is a charter of holiness, a theme expounded in the last eleven chapters of Leviticus. Love accepts us unconditionally for what we are at this present moment in time, whereas holiness prepares us for what we are to be in eternity: witnesses to the fullness of humanity in the likeness of Christ himself.

In the Law of Moses holiness has a strongly negative side; to separate oneself from what is morally or ritually unclean is an important aspect. As the way of Christ unfolds, so does holiness assume a more positive character. In Peter's dream, symbolic as it is, a great sheet of sailcloth descends, and in it all kinds of creatures are contained. Peter is bidden to kill and then eat them. When he demurs on account of their ritual uncleanness, he is told that he is not the arbiter of cleanliness. He has no right to call profane what God counts clean (Acts 10.9–16). Previously Jesus had taught that it was not what goes into a man's mouth that defiles him, but what comes out of it. What we eat obeys the natural laws of metabolism and is ultimately discharged in one way or another. But what comes out of the mouth has its origin in the heart, and this is what defiles a person. Wicked thoughts, murder, adultery, fornication, theft, perjury and slander all proceed from the heart, and these are the things that defile us (Matthew 15.10–20). In the flow of life we cannot separate ourselves absolutely from the elements of our environment, no matter how invidious to our propriety they may appear. We have, like Jesus, to mix with all manner of people in order to gain deeper self-knowledge, to develop a broader view of life and to help reclaim that which is lost. The process is dangerous – it cost Jesus his life in terrible suffering – but it is the authentic way of holiness. The spiritual life does not promise invulnerability; it does, however, provide an inner strength to withstand the assaults of evil forces and a growing love to embrace them so as to aid their neutralization and ultimate transmutation. A holy person radiates the love of God to us, so that the divine presence within us is kindled. Then we too participate in that holiness. It is in this way that love and holiness come together in a point of sacred dedication to God and man.

Since the holiness of God forbids us to use his name except in the willed ascent of the mind to him in contemplative prayer, should we therefore banish all direct thoughts of God from our daily work? Can the transcendent God of holiness be a possible source of meditation in our disturbed world of forms? The answer is, to the contrary, that until the holiness of God is a constant accompaniment of all we do in each moment of life, whatever we achieve will finally be consummated in futility. Man's own works founder on the rocks of decay and death; what God has inspired alone survives the attrition of time and place, illuminating future ages with a vision of splendour and a service that are timeless. But we have to move beyond the usual selfish demands for rewards and favours. God may be a 'very present' help to us in trouble, our shelter and our refuge, in the words of the opening verse of Psalm 46, but his help and concern are for all other people equally. He may be our special friend, but his concern is impartial and universal. The anthropomorphic god of punishment and reward is an idol who tempts us to cajolement and bribery. Nor is God, our timely, very present help, a dominating figure who watches us continually, rather in the style of 'Big Brother', so terrifyingly delineated by George Orwell in his prophetic study *Nineteen Eighty-four*. Such a constant companion would thwart and diminish us until all free will was removed and we depended entirely on his generosity for our survival. This mental construct is an illustration of the Freudian super-ego magnified and personalized to gigantic, horrifying proportions. Until this image is expunged from our minds, the true, nameless God will be excluded from our knowledge.

The essential teaching of the Wisdom literature of the Bible is, 'The fear of the Lord is the beginning of wisdom'. This fear is a holy awe, not an attitude of dread. Awe brings every faculty to vibrancy; it makes us listen, not only with the ears but with all the senses; it makes us psychically aware and intellectually taut. In other words, the fear of God awakens us from our customary somnolence and heightens our responsiveness. It makes us realize that we are witnesses and partakers of a mystery, whose unfolding is beyond our grasp, let alone our prediction. Perfect love banishes fear (1 John 4.18), a fear of being punished by the one we worship, but it does not decrease our awe for our Creator. Indeed, it deepens our respect for the mystery of each creature. Whom I really love, I respect and accord full reverence, even as husband and wife are pledged to honour and protect each other in the varied course of their life together. The rapt awe that the Psalmist articulates when he contemplates the wonder of his own creation is the most perfect love we can offer God directly, 'Thou it was who did fashion my inward parts; thou didst knit me together in my mother's womb. I will praise thee, for thou dost fill me with awe; wonderful art thou, and wonderful thy works' (Psalm 139.13–14). That love must then be sent out into the world as we regard God's other creatures with equal respect and delight, pledging ourselves to their protection and service in the name of God. When all people attain this height of self-awareness and self-giving, the world will indeed move beyond the slavery of decay into the glorious splendour of eternal nature. But this will surely also be the moment of the parousia, the second coming of the Lord who is always with us but whose presence is hidden from our vision in worldly consciousness.

Therefore our relationship with God is something more than easy familiarity. It is the full relationship of son to father, who most certainly sustains us day by day, but also makes great demands on us: 'there must be no bounds to your goodness, as your heavenly Father's goodness knows no bounds', as Jesus taught (Matthew 5.48). Our strivings after goodness are tried and tested in the school of experience, in which the light of happiness is complemented by the shadows of suffering. We are to grow into mature sons of God, capable of performing the work set before us, as Jesus did in his own life. Were it not for God's presence in our lives, no growth would be possible; once his presence is conscious, spiritual growth is initiated, and we progress to a full humanity, witnessed by the great saints of all the traditions, culminating in the work of Jesus. For this presence to be constantly before us, the practice of prayer is the essential work. To set aside a special period of time each day – preferably on a number of occasions – in which we give ourselves wholly to the practice of awareness in silence is the beginning of our deeper relationship with God. Prayer is not speaking to the God of our imagining; it is listening to the God of eternity as he reveals himself even to us. 'Thus speaks the high and exalted one whose name is holy, who lives for ever: I dwell in a high and holy place with him who is broken and humble in spirit, to revive the spirit of the humble, to revive the courage of the broken' (Isaiah 57.15). The first beatitude complements this teaching: 'How blest are those who know their need of God; the kingdom of Heaven is theirs' (Matthew 5.3). When one is aware of one's own nothingness, one is in a position to be filled with good things provided one opens oneself in trust and dedication to the highest one understands.

The experience of the presence of God has a mystical quality; as one is still, so one is lifted up and a fresh appreciation of reality dawns on one. We could never give a concrete name to this presence, yet it is one with which we can communicate in profound intimacy. It fills us with aspiration, hope and love. We can communicate with it in spoken or mental discourse, but in time such conversation ends in complete silence. In this silence, the divine presence accompanies us wherever we are and whatever we are doing. It neither directs nor dominates us; it is simply a constant source of strength and caring. As our prayer life grows with assiduous practice and unremitting perseverance, so the presence of the nameless one is always available to us, and is finally always with us. If we are so inclined, we can address this presence directly, but in due course we learn that such a conversation is at least as much to ourselves with the tragically divided consciousness we inherit as to the one whom we love with devotion and awe. Jesus' teaching on prayer is very relevant: he tells us not to go babbling on like the heathen, who believe that God's response is directly proportional to the volume of their petitions. Instead he teaches us the Lord's Prayer, reminding us that in any case God knows our needs even before we ask him (Matthew 6.7–13). When we pray in words and thoughts we are addressing the conscious mind through the unconscious, which is energized by the Holy Spirit. The conversation between the split portions of the mind is conducted in God's presence, so that in the end a closer collaboration is effected between the conscious and unconscious life of the person. As the personality becomes better integrated through inner conversation, so it can dedicate itself in willed, single-pointed awareness to God and his Kingdom.

As a truly spiritually aware person grows in experience so he becomes increasingly conscious of God's constant presence. God knows us and can direct us provided we have the courtesy to ask for the directions. This he does by infusing us with his Spirit so that every function of the personality is quickened and strengthened. In this way we begin to practise the presence of God during our daily work, no less than in those times given over entirely to contemplative silence before God, who is best thought of as he who is. God alone is the true *I am*, and the more closely we give ourselves to his service, the more certainly do we realize our own identity. We know him ever more intimately as we approach him in wordless devotion. This is the highest worship we can offer, and it overflows in devotion to our fellow creatures. It is in this way that we make right use of the name of God, whether or not we articulate the word. The proof of that immaculate usage is the transforming effect our presence has on those around us. It is no longer merely ourself that is present, but God also: the life I live is no longer my life, but the life that Christ lives in me (Galatians 2.20).

It may be questioned whether special times set aside for silent worship are ultimately necessary if we are, in practice, to be aware of God's presence at all times. The emphatic answer is that, devoted as we may be to God's service, we need special periods of retrenchment when we can give ourselves totally and without distraction to him. The world bears down relentlessly on us all, and especially on the saints who have an enormous psychic burden to carry; they would be utterly crushed were it not for their practice of rapt prayer in the silence of self-transcendence when they are one with God. Jesus himself had to fight for survival during his encounter with overwhelming psychic darkness at Gethsemane; his proficiency at prayer was of crucial significance here, as is recounted in Luke's account of the agony in the garden.

When we know God well in the silence, we remember his presence during the vicissitudes of a day's work, but we are even more thankful than before to renew our intimacy with him in the quietness of an open heart when we are alone. The end of our spiritual life is to be in constant communion with God, to pray without ceasing, so that his nameless presence is on our lips and in our hearts whether we are in the hectic thrust of emotional chaos or in the controlled tranquillity of solitude. The strength of our fellowship with God depends on our deep intimacy with him in prayer, and it is proved in the life of the world by our calmness, awareness of others and self-control in the face of great provocation. None of this is easy, but it is the fruit of assiduous cultivation of the prayer life carried out over a long period of time. On the unfailing presence of God in our life as a conscious power depends our ability to fulfil the moral law that comprises the latter half of the Decalogue.

'I will show portents in the sky and on earth, blood and fire and columns of smoke; the sun shall be turned into darkness and the moon into blood before the great and terrible day of the Lord comes. Then everyone who invokes the Lord by name shall be saved' (Joel 2.30–2). Even when the revelation of all things is near at hand, when the total destruction of all material objects is threatened, those who knew God in truth will be saved; perhaps it will then be their duty and privilege to save that which is threatened with extinction. This may be the ultimate hope in our time, poised as it is precariously on the edge of nuclear destruction on the one hand and life-denying political ideologies on the other. Certainly the divided consciousness of man is no match for these terrible forces encompassing us.

The conscious presence of God in our soul is the guiding light of our conscience, that within us which provides a moral imperative for right action. To be sure, conscience is not simple and pure in itself, being also an amalgam of conditioning we have received in our earliest years (symbolized as the super-ego) and the impingent thrust of group loyalty on which we depend for the support of our peers in an uneasy world. But transcending these worldly influences on our moral decisions, there is the voice of God which will never leave us until we have obeyed the deepest call to authenticity: to be ourselves even to death, which swallows up all worldly wisdom. 'What does a man gain by winning the whole world at the cost of his true self?' (Mark 8.36). This conscience, instead of enslaving us to the opinions of our elders and teachers, or shackling us to the contemporary prejudices of those around us, gives us the possibility to be ourselves as sons of the Most High, in whose service alone there is perfect freedom. The reason why the divine service sets us free is because it makes no demands on us other than to grow into the fullness of our own nature, whose end is Christ himself.

Jesus says in respect of using God's name improperly, 'You have learned that our forefathers were told, "Do not break your oath" and "Oaths sworn to the Lord must be kept". But what I tell you is this: you are not to swear at all'. The invocation of heaven, earth, Jerusalem, or one's own head are all equally vain if the inner integrity is lacking. Plain 'yes' or 'no' is all we need to say, indeed anything beyond that comes from the devil (Matthew 5.33–7). As we become open to the presence of God at all times, so he speaks through us and whatever we do is to his power and glory. Our integrity shines from us as the radiance of the sun, and we no longer have to assure others of the truth we affirm. In our civil courts the ritual swearing in God's name to tell the truth is a necessary safeguard against dishonest evidence. But we will never pass beyond the more subtle guiles of perjury until our consciousness is constantly illuminated by the presence of God. Then the Lord shall be the one Lord and his name the one name (Zechariah 14.9).

4 ❧ The Peace of God

'Remember to keep the sabbath day holy' (Exodus 20.8).

The human is about his business ceaselessly, but he seldom has time to think about the eternal things; of God he is seldom aware. He believes he has no time for religious speculations, and certainly none for worship, in a world of strenuous activity, crowded with momentous events and requiring his constant attention. Time for prayer is invaded by the busy routine of mundane activity. That prayer is as necessary for the welfare of the soul as air is for the body is a consideration that is seldom consciously entertained, since it does not impose itself directly on us in our working hours. But our agitated round of works grinds in due course to a halt on the rocks of stress. This shows itself in the guise of physical disease, mental breakdown, emotional upheaval and sometimes even in anti-social activity that betrays the high calling of humanity. All this is in the gamut of psychosomatic disorder as it afflicts us personally. But it can assume interpersonal dimensions also, so as to disturb family relationships and eventually overflow into conflicts with those who work with us. Indeed, this accelerating process can reach a climax in national disharmony, as among ethnic groups or between labour and management. It may culminate in a serious breakdown of community relationships whose end is war, whether civil or national.

This then is the bitter harvest of human activity that is not centred in the divine presence. It is activism, the obsessive need to do something at all costs simply to justify our existence and to prove our power to control events. Instead, we are controlled by the fruits of our labour and become trapped in a vicious circle of events that have in them the seed of fearful destruction. Since man working on his own sows the seeds of his destruction, should we rely entirely on God to direct our lives, remaining quiet and responsive but doing nothing that is not impressed on us from above? This tendency taken to its extreme position is called quietism. It is a heresy as dangerous as activism, for it denies the free will given to us as rational creatures, and leaves us open to any impulse arising from the unconscious and purporting to be divine. There are some groups of religious enthusiasts who believe that in their times of quiet meditation the authentic voice of God comes to them, giving infallible instructions that have to be obeyed. Unfortunately the matter is not as simple as this, for organized complexes in the unconscious can often assume a convincing leadership when given free rein, as can also indifferent psychic forces in the emotional milieu surrounding the person. We have in the end to do our own work; God will not do it for us. The old maxim that God helps those who help themselves is true, provided we have the wisdom and courtesy to call on God in prayer as we pursue our daily work. In our world God acts primarily through the human personality, or as the Bible puts it, 'God created man in his own image' (Genesis 1.27), giving him absolute power over the other creatures. When we consider how in fact we are made in the divine image, it seems to be in our ability to respond directly to the divine presence that we come closest to God. That response at its highest makes us behave in a God-like way, as it did in the person of Jesus Christ. This is the mark set before us, and how we meet its challenge determines the ultimate value of our life on earth.

It is clear that the divine–human initiative determines responsible action in our world. If, as Psalm 127 reminds us, unless the Lord builds the house, its builders will have toiled in vain, it is equally true that no houses will be built except by the enterprise of the human mind and the labour of its body. The necessity for human collaboration in God's scheme is a measure of his love for us; we are not mere puppets, but are partners in his great enterprise. On our response lies the world's future. I am convinced that if we will destruction, God will not forcibly intervene. But we hope his presence in the lives of at least some people will serve to avert a calamity in time.

In the strange story of the tower of Babel that occupies the first part of Genesis chapter 11, we have an account of a population of ambitious humans out to dominate their environment, perhaps eventually the world. It appears that God is so disturbed at the potential strength of this group that he confuses their speech, so that they no longer speak a common language and can no longer understand one another. Then they are dispersed over the earth, leaving off building the city with its tower reaching to the heavens that was their ambition. The most probable explanation of this sequence of events, parable as it surely is, is that man working on his own without deference to God soon falls into conflict with his neighbours. Love alone cements human relationships; where the insolent pride of human ambition is the driving-force, love is displaced by expediency, and the weak are sacrificed to the demands of the strong. In due course the society collapses into civil strife with a disintegration of the monolithic unit into disorganized fragments that disperse over the face of the earth, gradually losing contact with each other. Love alone can reunite the fragments, and this may take aeons of time to achieve; Christians believe that the reconciling work of the Son and the renewing power of the Holy Spirit have striven ceaselessly in the direction of reunion and healing, but much has still to be done.

It is therefore right that a certain part of our working life should be set aside completely for us to commune with a dimension of existence that lies beyond the world of commerce, physical labour and intellectual striving. Of course, the period of sleep that punctuates each waking day affords us some relief from the demands of labour, but in this state we are unconscious. It is important to have a period of peace when we can contemplate God and his many blessings in direct awareness and thanksgiving, at the same time enjoying those blessings. The fourth commandment enjoins us to do all our work in the six days of the week, but on the seventh, which is a sabbath of the Lord when he rested after the labour of creating the universe, we too should abstain from all work. This applies to our family, household, and animals and also to any alien living with us.

The abstention from work does not include spiritual endeavour; indeed, our spiritual life is fostered by its direct openness to the unseen world, for a short time unclouded by mundane concerns. In this way the minister of religion plays his part in leading his flock in worship, and all those who can sing lift up their voices to God in rapturous praise. As God, even during the Sabbath, never ceases from his work of maintaining his creation with life and power, so we too aid this eternal work by being especially open to the divine grace and sending it to all the dark places by the power of prayer. Jesus was not merely justified in performing works of healing on the Sabbath, but was in fact choosing the best time for this work. In the temple the presence of devout worshippers would have assisted him by their prayerful attitude: even Christ, Son as he was, needed human support, as is seen more poignantly in the Gethsemane sequence when he took

Peter, James and John with him to fortify him in the terrible ordeal ahead of him. They failed, because they could not understand what was happening – the spirit was willing enough but the flesh weak, a return to St Paul's lament on the divided nature of the unredeemed personality. Later on they did understand, when the risen Lord forgave them and sent the Holy Spirit down upon them. Nevertheless, their presence must have been of some support to Jesus during his earthly ministry, while they, in turn, were trained by him as far as they could understand his teaching.

Of course, not all Jesus' sabbath healings were done in the temple; for instance, he healed the man who had been crippled for thirty-eight years at the sheep-pool in Jerusalem. But I believe that the general atmosphere of prayerful observance that permeated the Holy City played its part in Christ's work, and this would be especially powerful during the Sabbath. This consideration also reminds us that a period of spiritual rest is not simply one of relaxation and diversion. On the contrary, it is to be devoted to God's service in prayer which finds its end in human regeneration. The Sabbath, like other religious rituals, can all too easily become an end in itself, insidiously assuming the nature of an idol. The impression gained from the gospel is that the Sabbath had a strongly legalistic character among the devout Jews. Indeed sabbatarianism is a feature of some Christian groups also, notably those with a fundamentalistic approach to Scripture. Once the Sabbath has assumed the quality of a rigid code of worship devoid of all lightness and joy, it soon becomes a prison for mind and body alike. To be sure, the less spiritual aspects of our nature may be repressed for the time being in the unconscious, but they will reassert themselves with a vengeance later on. They may indeed assume a pseudo-spiritual character of fanatical puritanism in which the pleasure of persecuting all unbelievers can present itself as a service to God. Man is often at his most terrible when he is a self-appointed defender of God; the god he is in fact defending is a human institution with himself and his colleagues as the preservers of it. The nameless God of reality is crucified as he was at Calvary. Thus Jesus taught that the Sabbath was made for the sake of man and not man for the Sabbath (Mark 2.27).

The value of the Sabbath can be related to various levels of the human personality. On the purely physiological level, the day free of arduous work, by which I mean work for wages, allows the body to be given rest. There are few more delectable experiences than that of giving oneself freely to providence in the knowledge that no active labour is expected of one. It is akin to the total relaxation of the body that is a precursor of the period of sleep. It also implies a trust in the created order of life, that we can rely on it absolutely and rest in its beneficence. If the six days of toil are our contribution to the life God has bestowed on us, the day of rest is his gift to us when we can be as open to him as a little child and receive his grace quietly without any disturbance around us. This relaxation of the body from the tension induced by the heavy labour the world exacts for success in a competitive society means that we can imbibe and enjoy our natural environment with fresh awareness.

Anxiety and ambition project our shaky confidence into a vague, shadowy future so that we lose sight of the one central reality, the present moment in time. It is easy to lose contact with the immediate situation while we distort our perception of it by projecting our fears and desires on to it. As a result stress builds up through our emotional response to the mountain of difficulty we conjure up in front of us. We create the mountain with our minds but eventually it assumes a reality of its own: all creation starts in the mind, as thought is the precursor of action, whether beneficial or detrimental. Blurred thought creates imperfect forms that can easily trap us into voluntary imprisonment. The Sabbath therefore has a valuable psychological effect in breaking the vicious cycle of unproductive thoughts and precipitate, obsessive action. It gives us a time for mental repose when our minds can be filled with more profitable thoughts as we meditate on the greater world of natural beauty to be acknowledged and explored, of enriching personal relationships to be enjoyed and extended, and of unseen reality to be sensed and revealed. It is in this last context that communal worship can be especially valuable, but it is merely the prelude to a more inward worship of God in the silence of one's own heart. Indeed, it must be admitted with regret that some forms of communal worship are deeply disturbing, if not offensive, to the more sensitive type of believer. It is for this reason that there should be, at least in our present state of spiritual development, a number of different forms of available religious observance. None is perfect, and perhaps all are eventually to yield to a worship of God in spirit and truth in the footsteps of the universal Christ who gave up his own life for humanity in faith and love. When this worship is upon us, the Holy Spirit will finally lead us to a full knowledge of God.

On the moral level of well-being, which is the experience of the soul establishing judgements of value in personal relationships, the Sabbath lifts us beyond the attraction of money and the enticement of power. It shows us the transitory nature of worldly magnificence and brings us closer to ourselves: what we are, what we shall become if we refuse to change our attitudes, and above all what will become of us when we die. At that great moment of truth we shall be stripped finally of all illusions, be divested of all possessions, and have to face ourselves as we really are. What we are will be shown by the truth of our relationships with other people and the amount of care we have given while we were alive in the flesh.

On the spiritual level, the Sabbath reminds us of our constant dependence on God, our gratitude for what we are and may become, and the necessity for prayer. Indeed, the Sabbath is a day especially available for remembrance of the divine Creator and communion with him in prayer. Since the whole day is available for recreation, we can offer ourselves without stint to God for healing and renewal. We are commanded not only to remember the Sabbath but to keep it holy. Holiness, as we have already seen, is an attribute of the Deity; it separates him from all that is unclean and corrupt; it emphasizes his transcendence of all human devices and passion. But in the form of his Son he visited the earth, taking on the nature of a man and becoming deeply involved in all things human. Therefore the Sabbath is not a time merely to avoid the sordid aspects of life in order to enjoy a welcome interlude of peace – if this were possible. It is even more a time to become especially open to the pain and suffering of the world, while simultaneously being grateful for the good things God has provided for us personally. The enjoyment of nature, where God adorns the smallest flower with radiant colour and illuminates the life of the humblest creature with a character all its own, is a spiritual treat especially available when we are not overburdened by the cares of our calling. The enjoyment of convivial company in sport, where the competitive aspect merely adds flavour to the informal encounter, is a sabbath relaxation. Since time is less obtrusive in its urgency on this day we can revel in the company of those we like, and share more fully in the lives of other people also.

From this we can see that holiness does not consist in separating ourselves from all that is earthy and enjoyable. On the contrary, it includes a loving participation in the things of the world, free of financial demand or personal aggrandizement. They are there for us to enjoy; we are there in turn to exalt and transmute the transitory earthly scene into something of immortality by our care and love of it. In the sabbath consciousness we become less aware of price and more of value; the former grasps, the latter transfigures. When we can glimpse the beauty in a face we had previously taken for granted, we begin to see afresh the power of God in all things. When we can enjoy our own body in exposing it to the renewing power of nature, we begin to understand what St Paul meant when he called the body the temple of the Holy Spirit. That Spirit is around us and in us, and when we are still in thought but alert in response, we know the Spirit, allowing him to transform us as we give of ourselves to the world in unself-conscious abandon. The Sabbath is, in fact, a time in which we can be ourselves fully and unashamedly. The end of the Sabbath is to bring that authentic person into the harassing world of commerce and labour, so that it too may be lifted up to something of God's Kingdom.

All this is summed up in the act of enjoying ourselves. In its popular context, enjoying oneself means escaping from the routine of work and immersing oneself in a round of entertainments. While there is nothing intrinsically wrong in such a period of pleasant diversion, and indeed it may form a necessary relief from the tension of earning our living and being constantly alert for the inroads of hostile influences, it is a shame that such enjoyment in fact bypasses the self and concentrates the attention on outer things. To enjoy oneself is to revel in one's own being, not in a narcissistic orgy of self-praise, but in an act of thanksgiving to the Creator. 'Thou it was who didst fashion my inward parts; thou didst knit me together in my mother's womb. I will praise thee, for thou dost fill me with awe; wonderful art thou, and wonderful thy works' (Psalm 139.13–14). The Sabbath is a day *par excellence* when we can look beyond the needs of immediate subsistence to the life of eternity interpreted by mindful awareness of the moment in hand. In this moment each phenomenon and event is a disclosure of God at work. In the celebrated observation of Thomas Traherne, 'You never enjoy the world aright, till you see how a sand exhibiteth the power and wisdom of God: and prize in everything the service which they do you by manifesting his glory and goodness to your soul, far more than the visible beauty of their surface or the material services they can do your body' (*Centuries of Meditation*, 1.27). After expanding on this thought he attains the important conclusion, 'Yet further, you never enjoy the world aright, till you so love the beauty of enjoying it, that you are covetous and earnest to persuade others to enjoy it' (1.31). The Sabbath is the time set aside for us to see truly and fully the world in this illuminated glory, when the power of God can touch us in undiluted strength, when healing can reach us from the unlimited providence of the Deity.

As a result of this changed attitude, we can respond in a totally generous way to the impact of our fellow creatures, whether human, animal or vegetable. And they in turn respond positively to us by giving us their very essence. The Sabbath opens up a vision that transcends the acquisitive quality of everyday life where we have to fend with grim determination for ourselves, and are dominated by distrust of those around us lest they get the better of us. The Sabbath lifts the occluding barrier of anxious self-interest, leaving us open to the welcoming love of God. From this love we can in turn flow out to all those around us. Losing our sense of selfish isolation, we begin to discover our identity in all things; being open to the perfect love of God in the holy Sabbath, we move beyond fear and enter a realm of heavenly trust. Indeed, the well-observed Sabbath is our introduction to heaven, which is best understood as an atmosphere of complete openness to God and to our fellow creatures: the love of God, of self and of our neighbour constitute a reflection of the Holy Trinity, which in turn directs our gaze to the undivided unity of the Deity.

The Sabbath is therefore the day when our mind can ascend to unimpeded enjoyment of the creation. This enjoyment extends to charity and self-giving, no longer in terms of duty, let alone recompense, but as a response to the joy within us. Life is a joyous experience, as the advent of each spring reminds us after the long barrenness of the preceding bleak winter. This does not mean that human life is easy; on the contrary, its punctuation with periods of trial and tragedy serves especially to illustrate the marvel of God's providence when once more the sun of beneficence shines and we can rejoice in our own nature. For it is the destiny of man to participate in the very being of God, as we read in 2 Peter 1.4, a promise shown in the life of Jesus Christ, and one in store for us also. What we see dimly now is to be fulfilled in the life of eternity, when death is swallowed up in the victory of self-discovery. This self can never die, and is to resurrect the entire personality, because the centre of this self is God. We make this discovery as we live dangerously during the week and at peace during the Sabbath. In fact, as we know God better, so the Sabbath consciousness pervades our weekday endeavours in an even flow.

It was recorded in Matthew's account of the crucifixion of Jesus that when he died the curtain of the temple was torn in two from top to bottom. At last the barrier between the sacred and the profane was breached, for in Christ even the most sordid elements of life were comprehended, healed and transfigured. The Sabbath, while concentrating our attention initially on the holiness of God, finds its end in making us increasingly aware of the holiness of matter, the creation of God. Two final insights about the Sabbath are worth pondering. The ancient rabbis used to teach that the Kingdom of God would come if only the whole of Israel would really keep a single Sabbath simultaneously. A teaching attributed to Christ from the Oxyrhynchus Papyri declared, 'If ye keep not Sabbath for the whole week, ye shall not see the Father'. As Jeremiah prophesied, '"If you invoke me and pray to me, I will listen to you: when you seek me, you shall find me; if you search with all your heart, I will let you find me", says the Lord' (29.12–13). The Sabbath is set aside especially for this inner work; once it becomes the power behind our outer work also, we will see the Kingdom of God.

5 ℰ The Family of God

Inasmuch as we all spring from a common human stock, each of us starts out from a home, however humble or inadequate it may be. We are all interrelated, and each person is born from the prior union of his father and mother. Were it not for the care our parents bestowed on us – cursory or devoted, according to the circumstances of our conception – we would not be alive. Life itself is precious; even when we are bitterly disillusioned with the darkness of existence as in times of pain and loss, we still realize in our better moments how privileged we are to be alive and how wonderful it is to share the glory of humanity, no matter how grievously it is betrayed in our daily actions. The culmination of this glory, to which all human achievement points, is to share in the very being of God, thereby to understand and enter into the mind of the Deity and play our part in the resurrection of the world. The gift of life is God's, but the medium of its transmission is the human organism. Thus the Word itself became flesh through the sacrifice of Mary. In her purity and selflessness she became the bearer of God the Son. Jesus did not spurn the maternal womb, and in his acceptance of incarnate life he lifted up all mortal flesh to the vibrancy of divine transfiguration. His mother grew in that pure humility which is a prerequisite for the unimpeded action of the indwelling Holy Spirit. The Church does well to venerate the mother of Christ and to pay special homage to the man Joseph who took on the paternal role. Without their love and protection Jesus might well have succumbed long before the beginning of his ministry.

It is an awesome moment when two people are committed to each other in marital union. Even more awesome is the moment of birth of a child conceived during the most intimate, self-giving moment of that union. When two people love each other in truth, they can lay bare the depths of their souls and become open to each other's vulnerability. Their self-consciousness recedes as their self-awareness expands until it comprehends the entire cosmos. At this moment there can be a divine penetration of the shared consciousness of man and woman, and the Holy Spirit can work his sublime alchemy in the couple. While all conception is effected by the power of that Spirit, the closer the trust and dedication of the couple, the more powerful and perfect is the operation of the Spirit. When we are empty of all desire except the will to give unconditionally of ourselves to God, then, in our poverty, we are filled with the divine grace; the riches that pour out of us show themselves in every good work. The birth of a child is a momentous work of human collaboration with the divine, perhaps the most sublime of all works. But how few of us see the process of birth in this light!

The family is the unit of civilized life. At its least, two people pledge themselves to uphold each other. As each gives of the self, so the other is enriched, and a new organism is established that incorporates the gifts of both partners, while supporting the weaknesses of each by the strength inherent in the other. Such a rudimentary family grows by the addition of children whose nurture extends the responsibility and caring of the parents; at the same time the offspring contribute their collective insights to those of their parents. Each person provides his individual gifts, while his shortcomings and defects broaden the sympathies of those close to him, making them more conversant with the wider problems of life and the ways of coping with them.

But in the family the two primary bastions, the father and the mother, hold a special place of esteem and affection long after the need for their support has waned. They are the symbols of strength and caring, of providence and devotion. Such is the ideal family as portrayed by the great spouses of antiquity: Abraham and Sarah, Isaac and Rebecca, Jacob and Rachel, Elkanah and Hannah, Zechariah and Elizabeth. Each gave birth to a child of promise, and we may be sure their spiritual support remained with their offspring even after their death. The memory of noble affection outlasts the physical form of its agents, strengthening those left behind with a practical ideal of perfection. This ideal assumes a psychic force which can inspire those who remember. It can empower them with superhuman resolve especially during the dark periods of trial and suffering that afflict the lives of most of us who are called to high endeavour. And in the end we are all called though few are chosen, because few can stay the course to the end. The spirit may be willing, but the flesh is weak. The inspiration of the love of those who have preceded us is a vital ingredient of the resolve that strengthens the weak flesh, making it in due course the body of a hero.

To be a parent is a noble calling; it embodies the virtues of faith, hope and love, and its joy is to witness the growth into maturity of a fellow human being. Its sacrifice is the giving of itself without reserve, and without any assurance that the child will either become a mature person or even acknowledge the love bestowed upon it. The two necessary qualities for fulfilled parenthood are devotion and non-attachment. The necessity for devotion is evident; its height is spelled out in Jesus' words, 'There is no greater love than this, that a man should lay down his life for his friends' (John 15.13). And this devotion, which may demand even the stark death of the lover, also requires the slower death of renunciation, so that the beloved may grow into his own identity unencumbered by the possessive bonds of the lover. The depth of love in renunciation is summed up in St John Baptist's assessment of his relationship with Jesus, 'As he grows greater, I must grow less' (John 3.30). No role encompasses this gradual, yet decisive, diminishment more absolutely, and more perfectly, than that of devoted parenthood. In the end the parent may become the helpless child who depends on the love of his adult offspring. This reversal of roles is characteristic of life itself, a paradox illuminated by the sayings of Jesus and more especially by his life. Thus the Son of God becomes the most execrated criminal on the cross of humans' inhumanity. The master is indeed always servant of all, at least while he is alive in the flesh of this world.

Our parents provide us with roots of security. They also mediate our continuity with the human family. They are, in addition, the first people with whom we may establish a close relationship of trust that should blossom into unself-conscious affection. This may eventually mature into love. 'We love because God loved us first' (1 John 4.19). The love of God imbues the parents with a love that outlasts all the vicissitudes of life. People with no spiritual pretensions will learn the meaning of that love when they rear their own children. Even our humble mammalian relatives show a touching devotion to their young which can put us at times to shame. Of course, they may also exhibit destructive tendencies, a situation seen sometimes in the human species too. The parent is an especially fine instrument of God's love because his life revolves around his children, at least when they are small. The children in their turn learn about God's love – and I believe there is an innate knowledge of God in the soul of all young children – through the love their parents bestow on them. It is for this reason that the relationship between parent and child is such a crucial one: on it depends the child's love of himself, of God and of his neighbour. Fortunately there are occasions where distant relatives or even strangers are available to take over the place of parents who have proved inadequate or who have been called away by death when their children are still small. The essential requirement is a focus of personal attachment on which the child can rely and to which it can hold fast in times of emergency. If this source of loving support is unfailingly available when we are children, we will learn to value it and eventually love it even when we are adults.

The relationship between parent and child is seldom an easy one. The parent remembers his child when it was a helpless baby, and may continue, albeit unconsciously, to hold on to that image even when the child grows up and has become an adult. On the other hand, the parent easily assumes the image of an insensitive, old-fashioned despot when he frowns upon the vogue enthusiasms of his adolescent offspring and tries to direct them towards more profitable ways of development. If the parent's devotion has been blessed by a non-possessive trust in the inherent good sense of his child, these storms of maturing can be weathered with comparative ease so that finally both child and parent may grow in wisdom through the shared experience of life. At the same time the two will learn to respect each other, so that the parent's love may pass beyond mere possessive concern to a delighted recognition of his offspring's native wisdom and gifts. In the same way, the child may see his parent as not only a provider of sustenance, but also a fellow human being with an emotional life not very different from his own. When one's parents have become real friends, so that one can discuss one's problems openly with them, the relationship has blossomed beyond dependence to a tender love that death itself cannot extinguish. By that time both parent and child will be on terms of deep friendship with many other people.

This indeed is the end of the parent–child relationship, that many other people may be welcomed within its fold. The family unit is the presage of the global family where all will be welcomed and none excluded from its care. In Jesus' very pungent parable of the talents, the servant who has invested his master's money wisely is commended, whereas the one who has let it stand idle is absolutely condemned. 'For the man who has will always be given more, till he has enough and to spare; and the man who has not will forfeit even what he has' (Matthew 25.29). The limited relationships we have in our individual families, if pursued with diligence and devotion, will make us more able to relate to the vast concourse of people we encounter in the span of an active life. We should not remain limited to our family, but rather extend the family ideal to those many different types of people around us who are not related by ties of blood. But first we must get our own house in order so that we have something warm into which we can invite other people. On the other hand, if we exclude others from our family life, we remain enclosed in our personal family; as its other members depart from us by the inevitable inroads of change and death, so we will become increasingly isolated until we are completely alone.

While the family is the unit of civilization, it can also be a 'little tiger' (to quote William Morris) that is concerned about its own well-being to the exclusion of any charitable impulse towards other people. The family is not an end in itself; like the Sabbath, it was made for man's benefit. Just as the Sabbath can deteriorate into a dreary, legalistic observance devoid of all spiritual joy when it becomes a tool in our hands, so the family may be rarefied into a gathering of the elect that divides people socially and intellectually. Just as the true end of the Sabbath is to extend it to all the days of the week, so the family finds its zenith and its completion when no one is outside its walls.

To return once more to the parable of the talents, the master says to the diligent servant, 'Well done, my good and trusty servant, you have proved youself trustworthy in a small way; I will now put you in charge of something big'. When we have dealt well with our parents in their dependence as they grow older, we ourselves qualify better to become parents to others. These may be first of all our own children, but later on that caring can be expended on other people also. The experience of bereavement, once the shock has been assimilated, can open up the life of the one who is left to a heightened compassion for many other people. Indeed, the family unit may need to be exploded by outer circumstances before the sympathy of its individual members can reach the vast mass of people outside its barriers.

Once we have experienced love, we cannot be complete until we give that love to all those around us. Love, furthermore, is unmerited. God has no favourites. This is the essential difference between liking and loving someone. We like a person because of his character; his traits harmonize with our own and we can establish common ground with him. On the other hand, we love a person despite his character. Love knows no bounds, and in its fullness it attempts to embrace everyone, indeed the whole creation. It is prepared to give up its very life for its friend, who in the instance of Christ is everybody. We are all so much a part of each other that there can ultimately be no assured happiness until we all participate in it. People cannot be changed according to our preference. We have to accept them as they are, and by our unremitting love evoke the divinity that lies within them also. This love may be repudiated, as in the instance of Christ among his contemporaries, and therein lies its tragedy. But it never comes to an end. This is surely the most important property of love in St Paul's analysis (1 Corinthians 13.8). This is eminently the nature of a parent's love for its child. This quality establishes love as the most important principle in creation, and it is perpetuated as the children become parents in their due time.

When we honour our parents we are paying homage to the qualities of devotion, sacrifice and integrity. Ultimately our parents become symbols of all that cares personally for us. Until we are acknowledged as persons we cannot function with integrity as individuals in our own right. We can form no stable relationships with others, and our witness becomes unreliable and eventually dishonest. It is the stability of our family background that gives us our first glimpse of personal identity. To be sure, this has to broaden to include our full place in the world, but the point of departure is the family unit of which we are at first the centre. Furthermore, if we honour our parents we are taking the first step in honouring common humanity. As we grow up so we bestow our love on other people also, but the stability and self-sacrifice of the parental relationship is our paradigm for all future ties and commitments. The honour due to a parent is imbued with flashes of thanksgiving. As we have received, so we in our turn can give to others. If, on the other hand, we have been deprived of parental affection, we cannot give loyal affection to others. To love another person requires first of all a love of one's own being, and this comes from God and through him to all in our company and primarily our parents. When we can take ourselves for granted we are immutably fixed in our own identity. Then we can flow out in constant warmth to the world around us. The stability of a loving family group is an ideal basis for this sense of belonging that fixes us in our own identity. To be sure, the identity expands as we grow, but its basis and uniqueness are unchanging.

The situation applies also to the country of our birth, our fatherland. It gave us nurture when we were small and helpless, it shaped the contours of our mind and its history moulded our moral judgements and our spiritual aspiration. Until we have grown to love our place of birth we will never love any other place. Love, in other words, is involved in each minute particular. It is different from mere goodwill which can remain a remote, often theoretical attitude of benevolence devoid of personal commitment. The man of goodwill thinks kindly of others and bears no malice, but he can remain comfortably detached from those who are in trouble while wishing them well. When he can descend to earth and lend a helping hand to his own inconvenience, the element of sacrifice is added. As he works selflessly on behalf of others, so love is kindled in his breast.

We know, of course, of the terrible consequences of undiscriminating patriotism, which is in fact an extension of exclusive family loyalty. All else is consumed in the fire of hatred as war ravages nations and destroys civilizations. Chauvinistic nationalism is the bane of worldwide co-operation, but it will not be cured by a vapid internationalism which refuses to identify itself with any country or people in particular while affecting to support all good causes. When we start to explore our own national heritage we can first begin to identify ourselves with the heroes of our past. We soon realize how interconnected all nations are by their common civilization and the religious traditions that lead them to an encounter with God. The mind and spirit of humanity move effortlessly Godward in the creation of great art and the establishment of scientific truth. When we realize this, we can thank God for the ancestors who made our own country and tradition great while extending that gratitude to the heroes of other countries and traditions also. These cease to be mere intellectual abstractions but become living forces within us. Then at last we can exult in our own tradition with such confidence that we are able to share it with other groups, while imbibing their national riches with equal joy. In this way a patriotic zeal broadens into an international solidarity where the strength of a country is evidenced by its capacity to serve the whole community of nations. In this state of being we are in all things, while the whole is comprehended in our individual witness.

At the same time a positive appreciation of our ancestral roots and national heritage should be balanced by a candid acknowledgement of the less creditable actions committed by our parents and country of birth whether at present or in the past.

This sober assessment prevents our gratitude proceeding to family or national pride. Honouring one's roots does not mean glorifying them, let alone deifying them. Praise that is not tempered by discerning criticism merely blinds us to our own less desirable qualities. If our parents are to be honoured, they should in their turn be worthy of honour. They need not be beyond human reproach – none of us attains this degree of perfection – but their sacrifice and loving responsibility should be such as to evoke a loving response from their children, at least when these grow up to a maturity which can view life from a broader perspective. Where no love has been given, none can be expected. In fact, the grace of God works unexpected miracles in the hearts of even the most deprived people who may respond to life with love despite its absence in their own family backgrounds. Nevertheless, the breakdown of family relationships on a large scale is an ominous sign of the disintegration of society: each person fights against his neighbour until the very base of civilization is shattered.

How in fact should we honour our parents? When we are small we do this by the act of obedience. Indeed, if we fail to obey them we will invite punishment. This is an almost reflex response on the part of authority to disobedience. It is a property of love to prevent the beloved endangering itself unnecessarily: a father who spares the rod hates his son, but one who loves him keeps him in order (Proverbs 13.24). In this way the parent brings his child into the protection of the society he is to serve. To obedience is added loyalty as the child grows up and actualizes his own gifts and establishes his own pattern of life. Meanwhile his own insights dawn and his unique identity develops into its full expression. Loyalty, as we have already said, is faithful support illuminated by truth. We should be true to our parents and friends without in any way denying their errors or ignoring their frailties. Thus we can remain loyal to our parents while blazing our own trail, which may be a very different one from that envisaged by them in their fond imagination. Loyalty embraces the qualities of obedience, affection and integrity. Eventually it matures to love, the supreme quality of relationship which transcends any desire, demand or duty. It is a simple, direct contemplative awareness in which there is total giving of oneself in silence to our parents when they are old, decrepit and possibly the victims of senile dementia. We too may one day suffer these indignities of old age, but as we have given service in our time, so will devotion be shown us also.

It is instructive finally to consider Jesus' relationship with his mother; how he loved her yet from an early age showed his independence of her. His primary loyalty was to his heavenly Father, as he made clear in the episode of his debating in the temple with the doctors of the Law when only twelve years old. His attitude to the very natural distress of his parents was incisive and clear, but it showed scant sympathy towards their human frailty. Nevertheless, he went back with them to Nazareth and continued to be under their authority (Luke 2.41–51). When his ministry commenced, his independence was all the greater. When his mother drew his attention to the lack of wine at the marriage-feast in Cana-in-Galilee, he told her not to be over-concerned in the matter: it was his business and his hour was yet to come. Nevertheless, he performed the miracle of turning water into wine, to be seen even more potently as a sign of the transformation of all the creation from insipidity to vibrancy in the presence of the Lord.

On another occasion his mother and brethren came to see him while he was in discourse with a crowd in a house. He dismissed their priority over him by observing that anyone who does God's will is his brother, sister and mother (Mark 3.31–5). Clearly the spiritual relationship we all share equally with God far outdistances even the intimate physical relationship based on ties of blood or marriage we have with special people. In the end all the world is to be brought into that intimate relationship as we grow in the consciousness of God. Nevertheless, when Jesus hung suspended on the cross between two criminals and no one was particularly anxious to be identified as his friend, the three women who remained silent below held vigil for him; in John's account one of these women was his mother whom he entrusted to John himself for care after his own death (John 19.25–7). We therefore see the balance in Jesus' life between obedience and commitment to his parents and a total transcendence of attachment to them. When he was young, he may well have been so absorbed in God that he found human dependence rather irksome. But when his full ministry dawned and he was drawn to common humanity in all its sordid reality and heroic sacrifice, it may well be that he saw his family in a much more sympathetic light. 'Son though he was, he learned obedience in the school of suffering' (Hebrews 5.8). This suffering brought him to full perfection, to a complete balance of the divine and human natures. This balance has also to be struck between the love we owe particular people and the love we are to have for all people. In the end the multitude merge with the family, extending it to embrace all creation, while all is brought up to divine participation.

6 ✣ The Sanctity of Life

'You shall not commit murder' (Exodus 20.13).

The usual form of this commandment is, 'You shall not kill', but it is assumed that the type of killing proscribed involves the wilful taking of the life of a fellow human being in the furtherance of one's own selfish ends. Life is God's most precious gift to us, and only he can withdraw it from us. To feel compelled to take one's own life is a grievous enough tragedy; to deprive someone else wantonly of life is the most terrible crime one can commit against him. Not only is his own creative future brought to an abrupt end, but society itself is also diminished. We do not live for ourselves alone, but are giving constantly of our own essence to others. This state of affairs applies not only to those people who have a joyfully creative function in life, whether in the realms of art, science or philanthropic endeavour, but also to the many who merely stand and wait. In the famous words from John Donne's *Devotions*, 'No man is an island, entire of itself. Any man's death diminishes me, because I am involved in mankind. And therefore never send to know for whom the bell tolls; it tolls for thee'. The basis of this communal involvement in all things is that we all are the parts of one body (Ephesians 4.25), and a single psychic energy infuses us all. If one of us behaves anti-socially, that person cuts himself off from a vital psychic link whose source is the Holy Spirit. Until he returns to the fold humble and contrite, so that he confesses his sin and asks forgiveness, he remains outside the pale of his brothers and excludes himself from the lifegiving power of God's Spirit. On the other hand, the act of contrition with the earnest intention of amending his ways in the future places that person once more in the full flow of the Holy Spirit as well as at peace with his neighbours.

In this instance the fault of one person weakens the communal solidarity, the trust we have one in another, that is the basis of civilized existence on which we all depend for our sustenance.

But when a person is summarily disposed of in the act of murder, a void is left in the society of which he was a member. It has been violated, torn asunder and dismembered by the forceful removal of even a single component, and the local social unit is irreparably diminished. This diminishing depends, as we have noted already, upon the unique essence of the person rather than his particular usefulness to those around him. Even if the victim is an infant incapable of contributing anything tangible to the community, its precipitate departure from the scene casts a shadow of chaos on the lives of those who are caught up in the tragedy. The mystic is always aware of a corporate solidarity that binds all creation together in the love of God. But in our world the human, by virtue of his massive intellectual equipment, has been given the power to weld the remainder of created forms into a mighty organism of purpose and development. Alternatively, he can destroy them utterly. Which of these two possibilities is to prevail depends on whether human ingenuity aligns itself to God in humble prayer or goes its own way regardless of the transcendent reality that governs all things. The first way is one of life and growth, the second leads inevitably to destruction. The wilful killing of a single person points to the consequences of the human being acting in disregard for the higher moral law which was given to us for our own protection.

That murder is an atrocious crime needs little further comment; few civilized people of normal mentality would disagree. The question, however, arises as to the scope of permissible killing of a fellow human being and ultimately the propriety of any killing at all. The matter is always urgent, but never more so than in our current intellectually brilliant society where mankind seems to have almost unlimited technological means at its disposal. It can prolong life for a long time where death would normally have occurred. On the other hand, it has terrible means at hand for widespread destruction of all living forms. Is it ever lawful to take another person's life? Alternatively, is it compassionate to prolong the life of a severely defective infant or an intractably demented adult, to say nothing of those many people with progressive, crippling organic disease for which there is no effective treatment at present available? Anyone who looks to Scripture for the definitive answer to these questions, in the frame of mind of a devotee consulting an oracle, is acting irresponsibly. We have also to use to the full the reasoning power God has given us as well as the deeper intuition with which we humans have been variably endowed. This intuitive faculty seems to be an essential quality of the soul; it is brought in at birth, but subsequently greatly developed in the school of life by the many experiences we all have to undergo. We learn especially in the depths of suffering, when, like Jesus, we are taken down from our own private seat of sufficiency to share unobtrusively with the milling crowds around us. The common people who heard Jesus gladly are our constant companions, and their wisdom is so easily ignored by the powerful figures among us who dictate the fashions of the age.

Scripture is not self-interpreting, nor is it elucidated purely by historical research, important as this may be. Its understanding requires a deep empathy with all life in order to penetrate the minds of those who were God's mouthpieces in past epochs. Their world-view was inevitably narrow and restricted as compared with ours by virtue of the paucity of scientific knowledge at their disposal. On the other hand, their awareness of the world of the spirit was far greater and more direct than our own because they were not diverted by technical expertise and worldly power as we are. We have yet to transcend the confines of a purely materialistic metaphysic, which sees matter as the only reality and physical death the end of all life, before the supreme scale of values may be properly assessed. Then alone will we be able to glimpse the eternal procession of life and its significance in earthly incarnation; then alone can we come to a spiritually informed understanding about death and growth into eternal life.

If we trace the biblical understanding of the sanctity of life, we find little compassion in the attitude of the Israelites in the time of Moses and Joshua. Sihon, king of the Amorites (Numbers 21.22–4), and Og, king of Bashan (Numbers 21.33–5), together with all their followers were ruthlessly exterminated when they opposed the advance of the Israelite community. So also were the cities and inhabitants of Jericho (Joshua 6), apart from the prostitute Rahab and her family, and Ai (Joshua 8). All this is done in the name of God who has put the cities of Jericho and Ai under a solemn ban. Thus a primitive people is supplanted by a much more spiritually developed community, and civilization advances. But we cannot help feeling disquiet, at the very least, at the extermination of an aboriginal people, any more than we register revulsion when we consider how European immigrants in the earlier centuries of our era rooted out many of the original inhabitants of America, Africa and Australasia. Western imperialism throve on the exploitation of such aboriginal peoples as were spared immediate death. But, as we know, the harvest of rapacious colonialism is not a happy one. The descendants, perhaps centuries later, have to bear the brunt of the injustices perpetrated by their forebears. And what is the fate of ruthless exterminators in the life beyond death? As the spiritual consciousness of the Israelites grew, so did their tendency to kill their enemies decline. The law of retaliation, an eye for an eye and a tooth for a tooth (Exodus 21.23–5), was in fact a significant moderation of the impulse towards indiscriminate revenge against a vanquished enemy; it limited the punishment to the extent of the offence. In the post-exilic period, when Judaism was being inaugurated, the clemency of the rabbis was well known. They shrank at the possibility of killing their fellows. Jesus went even further: 'You have learned that our forefathers were told, "Do not commit murder; anyone who commits murder must be brought to judgement": But what I tell you is this: Anyone who nurses anger against his brother must be brought to judgement. If he abuses his brother, he must answer for it in the fires of hell' (Matthew 5.21–2). The heart of these stern demands does not lie so much in the feeling of anger, which we all must experience from time to time in the face of obvious injustice, as in the act of nursing it in our heart It grows in rancour as it is held within one, and in due course is very liable to erupt in violence. There are other ways of effectively killing a person besides depriving him directly of his life on earth. A cruel betrayal of trust or a vicious calumny can so demolish the shaky identity that a person has built up precariously amid the hazards of life and his own imperfect character that he is totally shattered and his future career completely blighted, if not terminated in suicide.

Jesus, though the prince of peace, says, 'You must not think that I have come to bring peace to the earth: I have not come to bring peace, but a sword' (Matthew 10.34). He prophesies that he will be the source of terrible family dissension, for each person will have to stand up and be counted on his own. In another context, however, we read: 'How blest are the peacemakers; God shall call them his sons' (Matthew 5.9). It is evident that there is a comfortable peace in which falsehood flourishes under a mantle of easy complacency, the same complacency that Amos attacked so vehemently at the height of the power of the northern kingdom of Israel nearly eight centuries before Christ. It was soon to disappear with the inroads of Assyrian aggression. The true peace is characterized by the truth of God transforming the people into something of the nature of his Son. This comes in slow steps, but its end is definitive. Until it is attained there will be a war of attrition between the forces of selfish assertiveness and the power of the Holy Spirit which infuses the entire creation with new life. This life is of shared opportunity and devoted service to all. Selfish concern leads to conflict and death, the power of God lifts creation out of the cycle of decay and death into a life of abundant fertility and unending creativity. The Spirit is continually making all things new, so that a changed perspective on life is established among the people who live on the earth.

The law of life is evolution, which progresses by a process of natural selection: the species survives that is the fittest in the race of existence. By contrast, the inadequate are summarily disposed of in nature's perennial harvest. In the human drama it is well recognized that the majority of defective foetuses are aborted spontaneously in the earlier months of pregnancy; those that survive to full term represent merely the tip of an iceberg of congenital defect. In primitive societies, where the race for existence is close enough to death at all times, it is part of the scheme in many instances for the deformed and the weak to be left to fend for themselves, while the able-bodied move onward in the full thrust of life. Since life is God's most precious gift to us, it is not unreasonable that anyone threatening the existence of a fellow being is himself liable to execution. The crime of murder is so abominable that the strongest deterrent seems not merely justifiable but positively mandatory. When this observation is extended communally and nationally, it is equally certain that innocent, law-abiding people and countries should be protected against the inroads of powerful, aggressive neighbours. There is, in other words, a type of killing that can be justified in terms of self-defence, whether personal or national.

When the argument is extended, it is all too easy to condone the abortion of foetuses known to bear severe defects in terms of the greater good of the community who would otherwise have to bear the cost of providing indefinitely for an unproductive member. At the same time it could be argued that death is the kindest solution to a life of impotence and humiliation such as severe mental defect entails. The danger of this rationalistic approach to survival is, of course, that the decision is placed completely in the hands of powerful men, who become the sole arbiters of matters as final as life and death. Those who suffered under the racial theories of the Hitlerites earlier in our century know only too well where this tendency led. Even those of us who are less obviously deranged than the murderers of that time are too much the victims of our own prejudices to be reliable guides as to the survival of those whom we may regard as hopelessly defective. Man is at his most dangerous when he plays god; the current experimentation with transplanted human embryos is another indication of the danger inherent in technical skill without the awe due to the Creator of all things, including the human mind. On the other hand, man is at his most glorious when he works in collaboration with God because, in his devotion to the work in hand, he is transformed into something of the nature of Christ. Jesus said:

You have learned that they were told, 'Eye for eye, tooth for tooth'. But what I tell you is this: Do not set yourself against the man who wrongs you. If someone slaps you on the right cheek, turn and offer him your left. If a man wants to sue you for your shirt, let him have your coat as well. If a man in authority makes you go one mile, go with him two. Give when you are asked to give; and do not turn your back on a man who wants to borrow (Matthew 5.38–42).

Then comes the command to love our enemies and pray for our persecutors, for God makes his sun rise on good and bad alike, and sends rain on the honest and the dishonest. Even the wicked love their own kind, but we must have no limit to our goodness, even as God's goodness knows no bounds (Matthew 5.43–8).

These are counsels of perfection, but until they are prayed over, assimilated into our consciousness and become our rule of life, there will continue to be wars and killing. It must be said, in realistic acknowledgement of the human situation, that Jesus' demands are extremely hard. Not to resist the person who does you wrong is the vocation of a saint. Furthermore, even if we may have mastered our anger at an obvious injustice levelled against ourself, we could never lie passively when a fellow human was being similarly abused. This would apply especially to the maltreatment of one who was helpless, such as a child or a crippled person. Indeed, our solicitude would extend spontaneously to an animal which was ill-treated. An ethic which nodded at injustice in the interests of peace and quiet would be diabolical. We cannot, in the present state of human consciousness, forswear the use of lethal weapons when crime is on the rampage and terrorism threatens civilized values with destruction and a return to chaos. It is evident that Jesus' demands are compatible more with personal injustice and the need to transcend retaliation and work for reconciliation than with the terrible violence in our midst, much of which is a direct result of the evil actions of those who wielded power in the past as well as their present successors.

Indeed, the two events of our present century that cannot but mould our views on killing our fellow men are, first, the Nazi plague with its intention of total genocide, so that had it not been contained and vanquished, whole populations would have disappeared from the face of the earth, and secondly, the advent of nuclear power with its ever-present threat of total destruction of all life. The former event must justify the principle of self-defence with lethal weapons; the latter development makes all gestures of self-defence increasingly irrelevant in the face of a nuclear holocaust. Indeed, it is a dreadful thought that the nuclear deterrent has so far limited the scale of regional conflict and prevented any major war for forty years, a long time indeed in terms of the history of European conflict. Which of the two alternatives is the more acceptable, life endured indefinitely under an unbearably oppressive régime or total world destruction? The more deeply this appalling choice is considered, the more intolerable is either alternative. The first admittedly preserves life, but of what quality? The second hastens the death that is our reward in any case, but puts an end to life on our small but important planet. We can, however, remember the important prophecy, 'For behold I create new heavens and a new earth. Former things shall no more be remembered nor shall they be called to mind' (Isaiah 65.17), which is seen in vision by the writer of the Book of Revelation: 'Then I saw a new heaven and a new earth, for the first heaven and the first earth had vanished, and there was no longer any sea' (Revelation 21.1). The sea represents the dark, subterranean forces of evil, the darkness of the personal and collective unconscious. This does not mean that the earth does not count, but that attachment even to it can become a subtle idolatry, unless we worship God above all else. On the other hand, no one knows the extent of suffering that a nuclear holocaust would unleash.

One is forced to the conclusion that neither pacifism nor militarism is the answer to our unbearable dilemma. Pacifism is practical on a large scale only if there is a sincere will to peace with service among all people. While some are grasping for more, the remainder will be endangered if they cease to defend themselves, and indeed the situation of the aggressive groups will be increasingly unhealthy as they become objects of fear and detestation by those on whom they prey. Militarism is even less acceptable since it grows into a subtle love of weapons for their own sake, and often includes dangerous overtones of sadism. In the end it is the weapons that precipitate the minor conflict that could escalate into a nuclear war. The will of man cannot solve the problems inherent in human nature, any more than it is possible for us to pull ourselves together when we are in a state of mental disintegration. The panaceas conjured up by the human mind, though intriguing to consider in the luxury of peaceful affluence, do not work amid the turmoil of human suffering. Only a change of heart, a metanoia, can help us in our agonized, tortuous way forward to that peace which will put an end to killing our neighbour who, as the parable of the good Samaritan reminds us, is every fellow human being on the road of life.

Jesus said after he had made such apparently impossible demands that he left his disciples speechless, 'For men, this is impossible; but everything is possible for God' (Matthew 19.26). Thus we are brought back once more to prayer – not for God to bring peace to the world so much as for him to fill our hearts and minds with his peace. 'Peace is my parting gift to you, my own peace, such as the world cannot give. Set your troubled hearts at rest, and banish your fears' (John 14.27). These beautiful words of Christ in his farewell discourses are the true way forward to a society that does not kill. Once we know the peace of God that comes by grace when we are humble and silent, not only does that peace renew and transform our entire personality but it also emanates from us to all those around us. This is the healing power of the Holy Spirit which brings with it acceptance, trust and self-giving concern to all on whom it impinges. In other words, there will be no peace or security in the world until we personally can, in the footsteps of Christ, impart our own peace to the environment in which we live and work. How often do we encounter militant pacifists who seem to emanate hatred against those with whom they disagree rather than love to those whom they believe they are supporting! In fact such people are psychologically unbalanced, and are projecting their own unresolved conflicts on to those whom they distrust, whether in terms of politics or economics, and who become plausible scapegoats.

By contrast, the peace of God brings warmth and love into our hearts for all other people: 'Glory to God in highest heaven, and on earth his peace, his favour towards men' (Luke 2.14). It is then that we can glimpse the possibility of carrying out Jesus' radical demands about loving our enemies and praying for our persecutors. It is no longer simply we who are striving after the unattainable, but God working in us to make all things possible. When we have attained this state of consciousness through the combined grace of God and the work of self-giving in prayer, we can be emissaries of peace to those nearby in personal fellowship and to those far away in intercessory prayer. Even one saint can convert a multitude to the way of God; how much more effective is the united witness of many to God's peace! In terms of the precarious world situation this approach by way of personal holiness seems decidedly élitist and other-wordly. Nevertheless, it is the only way in which the consciousness of mankind may be raised from the bondage of self-absorption in mundane possessions to self-giving in life to the whole creation.

Much intercessory prayer in church services sounds as if we were addressing God as a distant potentate rather than the intimate presence in whom we exist, live and move. It is more important to pray that we may become peacemakers in our local situation, whether at home or at work, than that we utter eloquent petitions about peace and justice in foreign parts. Once our own house is in order, our psychic presence will effect far more intense intercessory power in the service of God and our fellow creatures than it will when we are emotionally distraught and mentally confused. Jesus tells us in no uncertain terms to remove the great plank out of our own eye before we start removing the speck of sawdust from that of our brother (Matthew 7.3–5); only then will we see properly. The tools necessary for the even more important clearing of inner vision are the practice of constant awareness of our own attitudes to others and ceaseless, devoted attention to God in prayer.

Then we will discover guidelines about such difficult problems as deformed foetuses, the incurably defective person, and crime on both a communal and an international level. We will see that all life is precious, a gift of God, and we have no right to terminate it summarily when its presence becomes a burden to us. Even the mentally handicapped child can teach us all important lessons in love, provided he too is given love and respected as a person in his own right. No circumstance is lost on the person who is aware; Job himself would never have had a direct encounter with God had he not accepted his suffering, albeit with a necessarily rebellious heart. But two additional observations must be made: the care of defective individuals must fall on society as a whole as well as on those closest to them in personal relationship. Since we are all parts of the one body, we cannot reject even the puniest member, let alone one that is sick.

Furthermore, our life on earth is part of a much greater scheme in eternity. There is a time to die no less than a time to remain alive in our body of flesh and bone. It is as cruel to keep a person indefinitely alive in a state of impotence and distress, when death would so mercifully have terminated this part of his existence, as it is to take away the life of a vigorous, healthy person in an act of wanton murder. The balance between life and death is keenly set, and it is understood and respected best when we use God's three gifts to us: common sense, intuitive compassion and the availability of his presence in constant prayer. We begin to glimpse the wonderful truth that our responsible decision in such a matter as life and death is the final common path of a decision in which mankind as a whole, the communion of saints and the ministry of angels are all playing their part under the guidance of the Holy Spirit. When we act as responsible, reverent people in this way, a great load drops off our backs and we learn, paradoxically, not to take ourselves too seriously. In such a state of joyous abandon we often do far more good than when we assume the mantle of God in trying to put the world aright.

Our work is to co-operate with nature, at the same time acting to fulfil its destiny by the grace of God, which perfects the natural order. Alternatively, it could be said that nature acting as it should reveals God's grace fully, and it is our privilege and duty to facilitate the perfect action of the natural order. Anyone who acts in wanton destructiveness to undermine the natural order must be checked summarily and decisively. Thus the criminal should be apprehended at once, both for his good and the safety of those around him. In undeveloped countries it is not unreasonable to demand the life of anyone who endangers the well-being of the community or kills another person for selfish gain. The deterrent effect of the threat of severe punishment cannot be denied. In the more developed parts of the world a kinder, more enlightened approach to murder should be possible. There should be less need for draconian measures inasmuch as the people are better educated and the socio-economic climate is more conducive to a truly civilized style of life. It is always a moment of great rejoicing when a society can support the abolition of capital punishment: it indicates that the instinctive reaction towards retaliation has been lifted up to a more considered response by insistent pangs of compassion, itself an awareness that we too have played our part in shaping the character of the criminal and that we must in turn bear his punishment. This acceptance of communal as well as individual responsibility leads

5. The Discipline of Love

us to explore the root causes of murder and to heal the criminal rather than simply to do away with him.

In fact it is extremely doubtful whether death settles anything finally; the hatred of the criminal continues to poison the psychic atmosphere, and it is very probable that the spirit of the executed person continues to live on in a hellish state of confusion that does no good either to him or to his fellows. This applies as much to those still in the flesh as to the deceased who now inhabit the greater world beyond death. Therefore it is in the greater interest of all that we should work towards the redemption of the criminal from his destructive tendencies while he is still alive in the flesh. A final observation is valid: we should not be ashamed when we feel anger, almost of murderous intensity, on hearing of a deliberate killing. This is preferable to a cold indifference with permissive undertones. But we should then master our wrath, thanking God that we too did not act as the killer did, and working with responsible concern to prevent the recurrence of a similar tragedy in our own neighbourhood.

The same principles apply to international relationships: constant vigilance should be informed by the ever-present possibility of a change in perspective. In this way friendship may lead to a transformation of our hearts of stone into living flesh. All intelligent people long for the time when mutual trust will be so firm that all armaments may be laid aside. Before this state of affairs can occur, however, nations must be freed from the duress of political and ideological tyranny on the one hand and grinding poverty on the other. Jesus said, 'If you dwell within the revelation I have brought, you are indeed my disciples: you shall know the truth, and the truth will set you free' (John 8.31–2). Jesus' revelation is that the Kingdom of God is eternally here, and if we dwell in that knowledge and direct our lives in accordance with it, we no longer depend on any of the world's idols: they drop like a dead body from us. We then need neither possessions nor power to implement our identity, but can live in trust with all people. Until we no longer need to make demands on others, and can let all people be free to live their own lives according to the insights God has set before them, and in a state of material security that liberates them from the threat of poverty and disease, there can be no peace in the world. Needless to say, these radical requirements are beyond human manipulation, but depend on divine grace working a feat of inner transfiguration in all our hearts.

Meanwhile we can give thanks for the witness of responsible peace-directed groups, notably the Society of Friends, who have exposed themselves to general abuse in the cause of pacifism. This refusal to take up arms has been determined not for selfish personal motives of safety but in a wide approach to world harmony. Their witness, minuscule as it is in a world of confusion, helps to lighten the load of aggressiveness under which we all labour. It must be said, however, that the Quaker witness flourishes most strongly in countries where there has been a powerful tradition of civil and religious freedom; the Quaker contribution has added depth to that tradition but has also depended for its existence on it. Its future would be in doubt, to say the least, in a bellicose, totalitarian society.

In the end our attitude to self-defence has to be pragmatic. Idealism is one thing in the comfortable halls of learning of an academic establishment or in the body of a church. In the hard school of life it has to be tempered by the harsh realism of struggle, subsistence, procreation and death. The more open we are to God in prayer, the more will our hearts, souls, minds and bodies be infused with the divine grace. Then alone will people cease to kill each other, whether by the vicious tongue, the scurrilous allegation or the lethal weapon. When we know love we will start to love all living forms, and will work for their healing instead of their destruction.

7 ᕫ The Sanctity of Relationships

'You shall not commit adultery' (Exodus 20.14).

Of all the Ten Commandments this one seems the most out-moded. Sexual intercourse is freely available to all who desire it, and the advent of medical knowledge has reduced considerably the dangers of sexually transmitted disease and unwanted pregnancy. The use of contraceptives is now widely canvassed as an obligatory precaution to reduce the rapidly increasing population throughout the world. No child should be born who is not wanted, is the general view of contemporary society; few of us would argue against this principle, but does it not justify promiscuous sexual relations once birth-control measures have been carefully applied? In other words, does the most intimate physical relationship that can take place between two people have no other purpose nowadays than mutual enjoyment? Does sensual pleasure, with procreation when it is specifically desired, define the whole purpose of sexual relations between people? If this is the case, it is reasonable, to say the least, to exchange partners as soon as the pleasure begins to pall; with someone else the delight may sparkle once more, and a new series of rewarding experiences may be initiated.

This essentially animal view of sex develops as our intuition about the sanctity of intimate human relationships wanes. Even couples who have a strong bond of affection often choose to remain unmarried so as not to be trapped by any ties of commitment. The threat of responsibility assumes the grimness of a mental prison which might impede that openness which is a prerequisite of fulfilled sexual intercourse. One-parent families, at one time a disgrace, are now an accepted part of our social environment. In a world that balances precariously on a cliff-edge of nuclear destruction on the one hand, and mass unemployment on the other, this looseness of personal relationships seems scarcely avoidable. As St Paul would parody the situation in relation to doubts about the resurrection of the dead, 'Let us eat and drink, for tomorrow we die' (1 Corinthians 15.32). If indeed there are no higher, more durable values, the most sensible way of life is immediate gratification of the senses: the end is adultery, lying, theft, murder and all the other degraded actions that together destroy society as certainly as does nuclear power wrongly used.

In the more traditional family life of the past it was the custom for couples to come to know each other during a period of engagement which culminated in a marriage that heralded the first sexual experience together in the relaxed atmosphere of a honeymoon. The snag about this arrangement was the not infrequent sexual ignorance of the partners with a clumsiness that sometimes marred the early period of married life. This might harden into an habitually unsatisfactory physical relationship, though more often adaptability was attained through patience as well as the exploration of other areas of shared delight – areas of the mind and spirit. Nowadays children are given information early about the biology of sex, so that few young adults should be ignorant of the facts of sexual life. All this is to the good so long as sexual intercourse is not reduced to a merely physical act. It is only when its full implication as the total giving of the one person to the other is realized that its depth and significance in the growth of the personality of each of them is understood.

How do we come to know a fellow human being? We can find out much about him by asking him questions concerning himself, his age, work, past history and his personal preferences. In the end we may acquire a plausible pen portrait of him. And yet we are as far as ever from a true knowledge of him. We begin to know him as we live in close communication with him; when we have gained his confidence and can start to open ourselves up to him, the barriers lift and he ventures likewise to reveal himself more intimately to us. Then we may see a very different type of person from the one we would have deduced from mere facts about him. It takes a long time to know another person well, even in a state of marital union. Indeed, we can hardly expect a fellow human to trust us until we are inwardly trustworthy, until we will respect him and guard his inner life as jealously as our own.

As we face our own inner being with greater equanimity, so we can accept another person more fully. As we learn to accept our own shortcomings with humour and honesty, so we can begin to love the foibles of those near us. We like what appeals to us, but life in fellowship is here to teach us to love all things, even when they irritate or frighten us. This is the love of God for us as mirrored in the love of Christ, who, as we have already noted, taught us to love our enemies and pray for our persecutors. Our subtlest enemies are the shadow complexes within our own unconscious; these are involuntarily projected on to people who irritate or threaten us because of their racial origin, religious views or social background. Possibly the greatest work of our life is the recognition of the varied content of the unconscious, coming to terms with the complexes and, through God's grace and our own fortitude, integrating them into a vibrant personality. In the instance of the great majority of people this painful adventure of psychological integration takes place in and through the company of a complementary individual, either husband or wife. Only a few can achieve this integration on their own, and they are the natural celibates of the race. Their task is to bring that integration to others which has been achieved in their own life, as indeed it is also the work of married couples who have attained inner fulfilment through their union.

The relationship of husband and wife is ideally the closest of all human bonds, since there should be a total giving of self, one to the other. No secrets are withheld for they are now one body, and life together brings to the surface the deepest fears and highest aspirations of each. The conjugal relationship, as we have already noted in connection with the love we owe our parents, is one of mystical depth. The holiness of the married state is beautifully described in Genesis 2.24–45: a man leaves his mother and father and is united to his wife and the two become one flesh. In this way there is a complete nakedness of soul as well as body, and there is no feeling of shame towards one another. It is evident that the marriage relationship is so intimate that it underlines the reverence between husband and wife as opposed to the tinsel of the outside world. It is a fellowship of truth, and in its perfection it can never be rent asunder, even by death. 'For love is stronger than death', as we read in the Song of Songs. 'Many waters cannot quench love, no flood can sweep it away. If a man were to offer for love the whole wealth of his house, it would be utterly scorned' (8.6–7).

We can, in respect of married love, contrast a truly loving relationship with one of mere usage. A loving relationship is one in which we give wholly of ourselves in child-like trust to another person. It is very different from the thoughtless, selfish contacts we so often make in everyday existence; in these we simply use another person as a means of discharging ourselves of our lust, anger, anxiety or prejudices without any concern for his welfare. Indeed, this lack of consideration for others, except in so far as it can appease his own selfish cravings, is typical of the life of the unredeemed person. Such an individual pursues an egoistical existence, living only for the satisfaction of his senses a moment at a time, without giving any thought to the long-term consequences of his way of life. To use another person selfishly is the betrayal of a relationship, whereas to give of oneself without reserve is the essence of a relationship that finds its end in the supreme relationship of man and God.

God's nature is always to have love, to be available for fellowship, indeed waiting in patient forbearance until we, his creatures, have had our fill of earthly delights and still find ourselves empty of substantial food. Then we can invite him in who stands at the door of the soul, knocking courteously for us to admit him into our life. He is always there but we are so seldom at home in our own being. When the excitement of the world's clamour has died away and we are at last at home in the silence of inner dereliction, we can begin to listen, hear, respond and enter joyfully into a relationship that has no end inasmuch as it grows in intensity until no one is excluded from its range and its welcoming embrace. This is the supreme I–Thou relationship in which we cease to be mere isolated units in a vast, impersonal world and become fully ourselves in the fellowship of all those around us. The mystery of identity is that we are most fully ourselves when we have lost concern for, even awareness of, ourselves as separate individuals in the greater concern for all our brothers; as we sacrifice ourselves for them so they too become more fully themselves. To be fully ourself is to live in the mode that God has prepared for us, a mode shown definitively in the incarnation of his Son. In St Paul's words, 'I have been crucified with Christ: the life I now live is not my life but the life which Christ lives in me' (Galatians 2.19).

What is necessary above all else for a deep personal relationship is faithfulness. This pledges a respect for the unique character of the person with whom we are in fellowship, and it shows itself in a concern that evokes complete trust. As a consequence of this growing trust, the one can lay his soul bare before the other, knowing that his most intimate secrets lie inviolate. The qualities within each of them that are less worthy are accepted and healed in the restoring embrace of love. In that fidelity my brother's secrets are mine also, I share his pain and humiliation, bearing his burdens while rejoicing in his triumphs. In this way, I become one with him in a deep awareness, as Christ is one with us in our personal pain and distress, no less than he was one with the common people whom he joined in festal celebration and later more poignantly on the cross of suffering. He had the capacity to relate without reservation to anyone who would receive him, and he gave that person the means to be fully himself. In the marvellous words of the prologue of the fourth Gospel, 'He was in the world, but the world, though it owed its being to him, did not recognize him. But to all who did receive him, to those who have yielded him their allegiance, he gave the right to become children of God' (John 1.10–12). This is the fruit of a relationship with God kept faithfully in prayer, and is seen most perfectly in the life and ministry of Jesus.

A relationship of trust does not consist simply in being able to confide the most intimate details of our private life to the one we love. There is also a constant exchange of psychic energy between us. The exchange of life from soul to soul finds its apotheosis in the action of Christ bestowing the Holy Spirit on the day of Pentecost on those who had kept faith with him, however inadequately, at the time of greatest testing. In the life of self-giving service and transparent honesty we become truly one body with those we love; in this unity the sacred mystery of each person's life is shared and exchanged. In our mutual giving we share each other's burdens, at the same time being filled with the renewing power that comes from the Holy Spirit. The principle involved in this transaction is fundamental to the spiritual life: the more we give of ourselves in devotion to others, the more available are we to God and the more open to his grace; the hungry he has satisfied with good things, the rich sent empty away (Luke 1.53).

Each intimate relationship is sacred; its holiness is due to God's presence uniting the two people into a single organism animated by love. But it is also necessary in the development of a loving relationship for there to be the human contribution of fidelity and perseverance based on mutual respect. The end of such a relationship is so complete a personal sacrifice that the other person may fulfil his destiny according to God's purpose. And yet as we traverse this path of self-giving, so we discover a deeper source of identity within ourself, an identity that becomes more vibrant with experience and is destined to withstand the inroads of death itself. This true identity is at once the spiritual self and the point of greatest authenticity within ourself that we have with all who will receive us. It is indeed the point of the soul where God is known, and through God, all his creatures become one with us. This point of God-consciousness is traditionally called the spirit; when we know this central focus within us and can work emotionally and intellectually from it, we shall never again be unfaithful in any personal relationship. At the same time we become fully open to the strength as well as the weakness of the other person. We share and rejoice in the strength while we give support in the weakness that prevents him from attaining a knowledge of God and of his fellow creatures and therefore becoming a complete person.

The reason why an attainment of spiritual knowledge, which is in essence a direct apprehension of the depth of one's own being where the Spirit of God is to be encountered, prevents us from becoming unfaithful to anyone is because in that knowledge we are in union with God and therefore do not cling to other support. At last our basic spiritual life is whole, and we can radiate joy and service to all who will receive us. Whatever relationship we make will be wholesome in quality and chaste in content: we give, not in order to receive but to shower blessings on all the world. In the service of God and our fellow creatures there is such a freedom from personal striving that we can live from our own being without self-consciousness, no matter what we are doing. Our very life is our gift to the world, in return for God's gift of himself to us.

This relationship of growing intimacy is the fruit of a marriage between two faithful people. Each has personal problems to face both alone and in the company of the other, but charity working in concert with honesty leads to the acceptance of differences, their confrontation, and eventually their integration in the life of the couple. The end is a relationship of union in God, which can be bestowed on the many people the couple encounter in their life's work together. Working faithfully together, they bring integration to all they do and to all the people they meet. God is with them at the beginning, albeit unrecognized amid the busy turmoil of daily life; at the end the divine presence is a very real support which can be called upon at all times by the practice of prayer. The paradox of a fulfilled married life is that although the fidelity of husband and wife is absolute on a physical level, their capacity to flow out in love to an ever-widening circle of friends steadily increases. In the same way, when we are punctiliously faithful to God in personal spiritual devotion, the charity that flows from us to the world around us is like a fountain whose waters are never stilled. The love we offer to God, either directly in prayer or in faithful devotion to our neighbour, flows back to us as an unceasing stream of spiritual power that brings new life to whomsoever we encounter. 'Bring the tithes into the treasury, all of them; let there be food in my house. Put me to the proof, says the Lord of Hosts, and see if I do not open windows in the sky and pour a blessing on you as long as there is need' (Malachi 3.10).

How different is an adulterous relationship! Here something coarse and unwholesome infiltrates insidiously into a fragile marriage relationship, which was gradually being established and fulfilled by the growth into reality of both partners through the vicissitudes of everyday life. The vows of marriage serve to consecrate the wills of both husband and wife to a lifelong union, and now the adulterous act seduces one of them away from the path of fidelity that leads to a life of abundance if followed diligently. Visions of private self-satisfaction are conjured up, and these can be enjoyed without regard for the other person. There is now set in motion the betrayal of someone to whom allegiance had been vowed. The soul of the trusting partner is violated, its secrets are betrayed and its mystery exposed to the common gaze. When the Israelites went after other gods they insulted the name of the one God who had made a special covenant with them. In so doing they betrayed the dedication they had previously sworn to the Deity, at the same time reducing him to the status of one among many gods. In the same way a betrayed spouse becomes merely one among an infinite number of people, an article of no special merit. That which is adulterated is falsified by a mixture of baser ingredients. This is exactly what happens to a marriage that has been invaded by an adulterer; it loses its spiritual character and becomes merely one transient sexual encounter among many.

Returning once more to the creation story, the great adulterer is the serpent who seduces Eve from her relationship with God by evoking desires of personal glory apart from the Deity. In this way she and Adam may become the arbiters of life's values without reference to the Creator. When they fall, they betray their precious relationship with God, thereby separating themselves from him. Their physical nakedness, once a symbol of their close relationship with God, now becomes a thing of shame that has to be covered before they feel fit to confront him. Their alienation from God and eternal life has become so complete that God gives them a finite span of earthly existence with death at the end. This is not so much a punishment as an act of mercy; to remain in conscious alienation indefinitely would be a far greater source of pain than the advent of death. Fortunately the hope of forgiveness and the prospect of growth into a new creative relationship of trust lies before them: the history of salvation, growing in intensity throughout the Old Testament, is brought to a triumphant fulfilment in the life of Christ. He alone can bear the full burden of alienation, bringing it to the Father at the time of his passion and death. In this way the sin of the world is accepted, healed and transfigured. But we have to proceed in the way shown us by Christ, a way that leads to a crucifixion of the ego self and a resurrection of the entire personality to the life of the spiritual self. However, Christ is with us on this precarious journey and the Holy Spirit strengthens us, so that what on the surface seems a doomed venture becomes instead our noblest experience. It affirms our full humanity, at the same time pointing the way to our coming to share in the very being of God, as glimpsed so magnificently in 2 Peter 1.4.

When the commonplace sin of adultery is seen in this cosmic context, its evil lies in its capacity to shatter a deep relationship of trust between husband and wife. The intimacy between them is invaded and destroyed and the growth of a precious organism is thwarted. Admittedly adultery cannot thrive in an atmosphere of marital intimacy, but where there is an unacknowledged weakness, the temptation to adulterous associations can be very subtle. The adulterer not only separates the unhappy couple by dividing the marital bed but also undermines the corporate unity of the entire family. The children are split by conflicting loyalties, sometimes being especially estranged from the defective parent whose attention is diverted increasingly outside the home. Parental strife casts a shadow of ominous insecurity over the happiness of the children, while the married couple drift further apart to become hostile strangers in a shared home. In other words, the act of adultery destroys the cohesion of the family unit, affecting the happiness and well-being not only of the injured spouse but also of the helpless children. The firm basis of a happy family life is removed from the children who become increasingly insecure in their own identity. Their sense of trust in their parents is undermined, and this uncertainty can be carried into their adult life. They may find it increasingly difficult to trust anyone with their inner welfare. Therefore an adulterous association defiles a beautiful human relationship, the state of marital union.

It would, however, be complacent and misleading to end the

matter on this high note of principle. Many marriages are in fact doomed to dissolution, and year by year the statistics for marital breakdown increase alarmingly. Adultery is nearly always a symptom of serious marital disharmony; relatively few adulterers are morbidly hypersexed individuals who cannot keep their hands off other people's husbands or wives. Such adulterers are in need of psychotherapy no less than their hyposexed counterparts who are impotent or frigid. The problem of sexual relationships is one of human immaturity, or rather, of asynchronous maturation. We are physically mature at the age of twenty, by which time sexual potency is at its peak. Intellectual maturity is also often remarkably well established in early adult life. Emotional maturity takes much longer to develop, often being rudimentary in scintillatingly successful people in the worlds of commerce, learning and religion. In most people a degree of emotional maturity shows itself in the later years of life when retirement sets its seal on the personal achievements of earlier active existence. We know an emotionally mature person by his calmness and his tendency to bring reconciliation wherever he goes. He has learned to control his inner feelings without repressing them, and he can deflect them into useful outer activity. He does not cast his emotional burdens on those around him by displays of sulking when he does not get his own way and anger when he is crossed. On the contrary, he is able to lift the emotional burdens of other people. If only marriages could take place among emotionally mature people there would be neither adultery nor divorce! In fact, however, the deeper purpose of marriage is to bring the couple into a state of emotional maturity.

Marriages may be made in heaven but they have to be worked out in quiet perseverance while we are on earth. The immediate delights of physical intimacy are brought into a more durable context with the rearing of a family. But if the edifice is to stand the test of time, remembering the greatly increased life-expectancy in the developed countries of the West nowadays, there must be a foundation of emotional stability, so that husband and wife can stay rock-like in their own integrity. While there must be a total sharing on one level, each must also learn to live a separate, independent life, both developing their own particular gifts and cultivating their own interests and friendships. Not only is this individual development essential for the emotional growth of each of them, but it also gives the one an emotional independence in preparation for the death of the other. Only in an atmosphere of complete trust can this individual self-actualization occur within the sanctity of the marriage relationship. Furthermore, this essentially adult growth of personality can thrive only in an environment of deep spiritual understanding.

At the end of the Sermon on the Mount Jesus asks, 'What then of the man who hears these words of mine and acts upon them? He is like a man who had the sense to build his house on rock' (Matthew 7.24). It is the movement towards spiritual maturity that alone can preserve a marriage from the temptations of the world. Adultery starts in the mind. Jesus said, 'You have learned that they were told, "Do not commit adultery". But what I tell you is this: If a man looks upon a woman with a lustful eye he has already committed adultery with her in his heart' (Matthew 5.27–8). The way to prevent this lustful gaze is to direct the inner eye of the soul heavenward in prayer. This prayer is one of contemplation of the divine reality, not of petition to God to deliver us from all earthly temptations. When our priorities are spiritual we can encounter and transcend the temptations of common life, for they cannot be permanently evaded unless we abdicate our presence from the world. And worldly life is essential for our spiritual growth. The way was shown by Jesus, who after his baptism was led by the Holy Spirit into the wilderness to confront worldly vanity and master it by his humility and obedience to God. 'The lamp of the body is the eye. If your eyes are sound, you will have light for your whole body; if your eyes are bad, your whole body will be in darkness. If then the only light you have is darkness, the darkness is doubly dark' (Matthew 6.22–3). Just as healthy, well-focused eyes take in the light of the sun, so the soul turned to God in prayer is filled by his uncreated light, which illuminates the whole personality, drawing the person closer to the divine presence. As he lives this new life in God, so the divine light emanating from him initiates dramatic changes in the people close to him, bringing them closer to God also.

The wise person delays marriage until he has attained sufficient intellectual and emotional balance to judge clearly how he wishes to order his life. The practice of self-control, which is the last fruit of the Spirit (Galatians 5.22), should govern all physical explorations of sex until there is a deep love for the other person. This love is something more than a feeling of warm affection, which will all too probably prove fleeting and insubstantial when another attractive individual arrives on the scene. Love brings with it a sense of deep responsibility for that person's welfare. Love is the supreme act of the human will, and self-control is one side of the coin of love; it is centred on the striving for harmlessness. The reverse side of the coin of love is total self-giving – physical, emotional and spiritual – after vows of permanent loyalty have been made in marriage. The practice of continence outside marriage is not a reversion to the radical repression of pleasure-seeking instincts that characterizes religious puritanism. It is an act of will that leads the human being past his animal ancestry to a full participation in his spiritual heritage. The will, when freed from the domination of the prince of this world, is the authentic action of the soul. To act from a centre of free will is one of God's greatest gifts to the human being. When we align that will to God in prayer, our will and the divine will act in collaboration. Then at last we begin to live from a centre of spirituality which governs and enlightens the animal part of our inheritance. Our response to the deep sexual longings within us determines whether we live truly human lives of responsibility or merely animal lives of irrepressible desire. The first is arduous, but it brings us up to that full humanity shown definitively in the life of Jesus. The second is pleasurable, but its end is a debasement of human personality, betrayed relationships, and a dissipation of potentialities into futility as age and incapacity claim their part in our lives.

'Enter by the narrow gate. The gate is wide that leads to perdition, there is plenty of room on the road, and many go that way; but the gate that leads to life is small and the road is narrow, and those who find it are few' (Matthew 7.13–14). The gate that leads to life is narrow because it will accommodate the person alone; those laden with the luggage of worldly desires are barred from entrance. Only the spiritually poor, those who know their need of God, have the Kingdom of Heaven (Matthew 5.3). Once one knows one's need of God, one can put all worldly desires into proper perspective by an act of will. Well attested is the psychological observation that when the will and the imagination come into conflict, it is the imagination that triumphs. When the imagination is filled with God's presence, worldly desires cease to impinge on it, and the will can act unimpeded.

When sexual intercourse is recognized as a sacrament of God's love for all his creatures, it will have ascended from its customary place as a physical activity of pleasure and emotional release to the way of growth of the human to full emotional maturity and spiritual knowledge.

8 ∾ The Stewardship of Resources

'You shall not steal' (Exodus 20.15).

The temptation to get something for nothing is strong in all of us. To the uninitiated the miracles of Christ fall into this category; little do they know how much it cost him to provide for the welfare of his compatriots. God's grace to us is free, but he gives of himself eternally to us.

Stealing is the way of gaining an unearned commodity by directly appropriating for our own use something that does not belong to us. It is usually a possession of another person or some communal property, but it can also be another person's ideas which we then pass off as our own in the act of plagiarism. The end of stealing is always the same; someone else is diminished unlawfully while the thief gains at his victim's expense. The prohibition is expanded in Leviticus 19.11, 'You shall not steal; you shall not cheat or deceive a fellow countryman'. As the moral consciousness of the Israelites matures, so the concept of a fellow countryman widens to embrace all neighbours, whom Jesus identifies in the parable of the good Samaritan as anyone we may encounter on the path of life.

The spiritual havoc encompassed by an act of dishonesty has already been spelled out in respect of murder: we are all parts of the one body of humanity, and an act that injures even one individual has its wider repercussions on the whole community. The victim, deprived of an article that belonged to him, is not merely inconvenienced to a greater or lesser extent depending on the value of what was appropriated. The act of theft leaves a gaping wound in the inner life of the one who has been cheated, his security has been violated, and he is subtly diminished in his self-regard. This is especially well seen in the victim of a confidence trickster, who has manoeuvred his way with heartless abandon into another person's inner sanctuary of trust, only to defile it when he absconds with the money or the precious article he coveted. It is this he valued and not the person of his victim who becomes like a discarded article of clothing. Indeed, the wretchedness of a theft does not depend only on the financial loss sustained; its deeper implications emit reverberations that disturb the inner life of the victim, producing a sense of violation. Likewise, the horror of a burglary is often out of all proportion to the goods stolen; a most unpleasant psychic presence contaminates the atmosphere of the premises that cannot be attributed merely to the physical disturbance effected by the intruder ransacking his victim's possessions. It may require some time to elapse before peace descends on the violated property no less than in the heart of the owner.

All this is as it should be; it does not necessarily point to an attachment to property so much as to the interconnectedness of the whole created order. It is not reprehensible to attach value to our possessions; on the contrary, it is a sin of omission to neglect any aspect of the world around us. Our very clothing is in effect an extension of the physical body it covers, just as our homes and the vehicles we use serve to house that same body and enhance its mobility for the many demands that are placed upon it. Likewise, money has its own integrity, and its correct use is one of the basic lessons we are called on to learn in this life. Neither money nor possessions can be taken with us to the life we inherit after death, therefore we are ill-advised to cling to them selfishly. Indeed, the accumulation of riches even in this world soon assumes the subtle form of a gilded prison which focuses an increasing amount of our attention on to matters of insurance and self-protection against the assaults of thieves and the inclemency of the elements. 'Do not store up for yourselves treasure on earth, where it grows rusty and moth-eaten, and thieves break in to steal it. Store up treasure in heaven, where there is no moth and no rust to spoil it, no thieves to break in and steal. For where your treasure is, there will your heart be also' (Matthew 6.19–20).

On the other hand, money and property are facts of material life, no less than human relationships, and their necessity will not be dispelled by our refusing to handle them. It is what we do with the things of this world that counts; rejecting them is an aspect of denying life, which may superficially appear to be spiritually enlightened, but in fact separates us from a proper relationship with the earth. Life cannot be divided into compartments, some of which are sacred and some profane. The incarnation of Christ and his death saw the curtain of the temple torn in two from top to bottom; from henceforth the sacred mixed freely with the profane, as Jesus had done during his time on earth with the many different types of people he encountered, in order to raise up the profane to true sanctity. In the same way we have to come to terms with life as a whole; effecting a proper relationship with things and events no less than with people is as much for our own spiritual growth as for the glorification of the material universe.

What we handle with reverence we bring closer to God; this is a function of the universal priesthood bestowed on humanity and performed most solemnly and splendidly in the consecration of the elements of the Eucharist. However, what is brought about in that great moment of the sacrament of Christ's self-giving to us for our redemption from the power of sin and our resurrection to a new life of spiritual awareness, has to be repeated in all our lives by personal holiness and a deep caring for the world's creatures. The violence of theft is the very antithesis of reverence – it contaminates all it touches in the act of separating the property from the care of its owner. The object stolen becomes a mere article to satisfy the covetousness of the thief. When we live according to brute nature unredeemed by grace, we inevitably make selfish use of the things of this world; needless to say, in so doing we have only a shortsighted understanding of what is most advantageous for us. This is an I–It relationship of selfish convenience, and if it is pursued remorselessly among the things of the world, it overflows into human relationships also. By contrast, when the Word of God lives in us and directs us beyond selfish concern to a sharing with the whole world, love flows freely from us to the people around us and also to the objects whose existence we customarily take for granted, but without thanks, let alone reverence.

A spiritually alive person is aware of the holiness of matter, because God created it; whatever God created is fundamentally good, but his rational creatures, to whom he has given executive power in this world, will tend to corrupt it if they separate themselves from the divine grace. This they do by an attitude of insolent pride which shows itself in a negligent attitude towards prayer, our unfailing means of direct communication with the divine. This applies especially to the practice of inner fellowship with God in silence, which is called contemplation. The spiritual person rejoices in the material world as he conserves the resources of nature with child-like wonder and adult resolution. By contrast, an I–It relationship is selfish, predatory and eventually destructive. This defines exactly the final result of stealing something: the article is easily damaged and its value undermined in a way not altogether dissimilar to the person who is seduced and lowered from the pedestal of chastity to the common floor of lustful expediency. That theft is unacceptable is confirmed by the world's great religious codes. Nevertheless, there are circumstances when it would be hard to resist the temptation to steal. Until we are provided with the necessities of life it is not reprehensible for us to grasp at our own survival and that of our family. The basic needs for any animal are food and shelter, without which life is impossible. To these elementary requirements the drive for procreation must be added so that the life of the species may be safeguarded. In an especially highly developed group like the human family, once these basic needs have been satisfied, there are more personal requirements to be met. Each of us is an individual in his own right, a fact of human life that should be acknowledged. Therefore the basic animal needs have to be humanized by warm interpersonal relationships and an acceptance of each individual as valuable, indeed unique, in his own environment. Our value as persons is reflected by the love that is our due from those in close family relationship to us and from the esteem we evoke in our social environment. This in turn depends on the value of the work we do and our general contribution to the life of our local community. This compendium of human needs is not by any means complete; it simply defines a sound foundation for personal and communal life. On this foundation a spiritual edifice can be built, since the truly human place is with God as collaborator in the building of the world. Our souls know no lasting peace until they rest in God's eternal creativity.

It is tempting and disconcertingly easy, in a flourish of idealistic enthusiasm, to meditate ecstatically on the final end of mankind restored in the divine image while neglecting the material and emotional foundation on which this great spiritual plan is to unfold. Certainly our present era cannot be accused of falling into this particular error. Schemes for social justice abound, at least in the more developed countries of our world, and in them a great deal of the harshest poverty and material degradation has been considerably mitigated. For this we should be heartily thankful, while working without rest towards a similar amelioration in the larger, less developed part of the world where dehumanizing poverty still afflicts vast populations. Without basic social justice civilized living is all but impossible, and as civilization crumbles, so the commandments of God's law are transgressed more frequently until there is absolute social disintegration with anarchy. Nevertheless, man cannot live on bread alone; he lives by every word that God utters (Deuteronomy 8.3). This teaching was repeated by Jesus to the devil when he was challenged to turn stones into bread. Jesus was later to perform miracles of supply far in excess of this, but this was for the sake of others, not his own self-aggrandizement. Furthermore, in every miracle he was not only the agent but also the victim. He gave unstintingly of himself that others might be healed, that they too might glimpse the Kingdom of God. The work of Christ is the direct antithesis of theft. 'For you know how generous our Lord Jesus Christ has been: he was rich, yet for your sake he became poor, so that through his poverty you might become rich' (2 Corinthians 8.9). As in all life, a balance has to be struck between the material and the spiritual for the enrichment of both.

Can it be wrong for a distracted parent faced with grinding poverty to steal for the sake of his starving family? The approach to this terrible situation, which must be practical if it is to be spiritually sound, is that we are all parts of the one body of humanity, and that it is unacceptable for any individual to lie derelict on a scrap-heap of poverty while others flourish, perhaps in idleness, on a comfortable income that may be largely unearned. But theft is an unacceptable way of countering this injustice, even if dire necessity may make it apparently immediately permissible. The act of stealing serves to disrupt even further the uneasy flow of social relationships, bringing in its train chaos and fear as part of a destructive impulse against the law of the land. Two wrongful actions, in this case social injustice and personal theft, do not cancel each other out and make for righteousness. If the thief were to succeed in his anti-social activity, his way would be open to becoming increasingly dishonest until he precipitated serious communal disorder. In so doing, he would drift away from the common good, however imperfect this might be, until he became a creature apart, an outlaw. Such a state of hostile separation from one's fellow creatures is a good introduction to hell, which finds its fullness in the total isolation of the individual from his fellows and from the knowledge of God.

The tendency to steal is a manifestation of an inner desolation: what the person lacks in himself he attempts to appropriate from others. This lack may be the result of a callous, uncaring society in which the person lives or it may be an intrinsic defect in the person himself. The two often reinforce each other. It is common for children deprived of love in their family associations, or who feel that they are the victims of injustice, to steal from those around them. If we return to Leviticus 19.11, we are forbidden to steal or to cheat or deceive a neighbour. In this instance, the child, deprived of affection, has in no uncertain way been cheated of a vital relationship with its family, and its response is a protest against this injustice. It is in effect a distress signal that must be heard at once for the sake of the family no less than the child; each member makes its own unique contribution to the community when it is properly integrated into it, whereas its own disintegration weakens those around it. In the same way, an impoverished adult who takes to crime may have been cheated of family solidarity, effective education, and a chance to engage in constructive work by an unfair social system. However, in this instance, the situation is nearly always complicated by the offender's defective character. Poverty, at least in the world's more developed countries, is due as often to the improvident use of resources as to a lack of opportunity. Large amounts of money are wasted on trivial entertainments and squandered on vice in so many societies lacking any vital spiritual directives, whereas some defective people vegetate in idleness. The personal weakness that leads to poverty, apathy and crime has a strongly moral component which is often aggravated by social unrest. Until the person comes to himself and acknowledges the source of the problem in undistorted awareness, he will continue to steal until he finds himself placed outside the community as an habitual criminal. It is evident that the tendency to steal is close to the divided consciousness we all inherit; few of us have escaped the implications of theft both as offenders and victims. The increasing level of world unemployment is bound to increase the amount of stealing even if the amount of money paid out to those without work is sufficient to obviate poverty. Idle hands herald moral deterioration that leads to various anti-social activities.

Stealing, in fact, begins insidiously with a subversive attitude of mind in which we give short measure of ourselves for what life has given us. The rewards of a human existence are a vigorous body, an active, intelligent mind, a warm, expressive emotional life and a deeper self, or soul, that can know God directly by intuition strengthened by the assiduous practice of prayer. Even if some of these human qualities are dim, we have much to acknowledge in thanksgiving. The privilege of a healthy body is all too often overlooked until we fall victim to a serious malady, just as a balanced emotional life is taken for granted until the advent of a mental illness or a severe outer misfortune. The payment that is expected of us for the wonder of our incarnation is ourselves alone. But whereas the financial demands of the world impoverish us, the payment that is part of spiritual development involves no invoices for services rendered, nor is there any sacrifice of resources. On the contrary, we gain as we give of ourselves, growing in the stature of a world benefactor. As we give of ourselves, so we are filled with the Holy Spirit who renews our personality and brings us closer to a direct knowledge of God.

We live according to the law of God, which is the divine moral order, when we give unstintingly of ourselves in service whenever we are asked. Often the service has a pecuniary reward attached to it, and we move beyond shabby, unobtrusive theft to a whole-some, giving relationship with those who are employing us when we fulfil our part of the contract with punctilious honesty. But sometimes there is no contract. Here we are working on God's behalf, and it is our privilege to give something of ourself for no material reward whatsoever. As we give fully of ourself to another person, so we fill him with something of God that has come to us. This is the Holy Spirit who flows out from us in free fellowship whenever we are fully open to the thrust of life whose creator is God himself. The more closed we are to life, the more do we tend to secrete our own gifts until they remain attached as inert, atrophied appendages to our puny personality. On the other hand, the more open we are, the more we are replenished by the Holy Spirit and the less is the temptation to steal from life's passing show. It is in this illumined spirit that we can begin to grasp the high teaching of Jesus about detachment and charity. 'If a man wants to sue you for your shirt, let him have your coat as well. If a man in authority makes you go one mile, go with him two. Give when you are asked to give, and do not turn your back on a man who wants to borrow' (Matthew 5.40–2).

The attitude that counters any temptation to steal is one of blessing. When we can flow out to life in a spirit of affirmation and an attitude of benediction, we are giving ourselves without reserve to all that we encounter, whether good or bad, favourable or unfavourable. This is the supreme act of self-giving that is evoked by a knowledge of God, and it makes tolerable even life's most terrible experiences. Thus there have been nameless saints of our own century who, suffering appallingly in prison camps, have refused to counter evil with hatred. Instead, they went about in child-like faith, relating positively to all those around them, and attained spiritual mastery. Most were killed along with their unenlightened brethren, like Christ crucified between two criminals, but their death was a great victory of the spirit of eternal life over material darkness. By their example working beyond the limitation of time and space, we too are encouraged and lifted up to noble purpose when all around us is dark and full of evil forebodings. While the way of theft seeks to evade this ultimate personal exposure by illicit material means, the way of blessing takes every circumstance aboard with it, and brings the collective whole to God, who alone can receive and heal it.

There are mysteries of grace in situations of intense terror and deprivation, especially when they are shared communally. When all our lives are in imminent peril, we tend to move beyond thoughts of possessions, rights and special privileges and enter more fully into the lives of those around us. Instead of contrasting our own lot, either favourably or unfavourably, with that of others, we seek to join our lot with theirs for the common good. Theft flourishes especially in societies where there is a great spectrum of wealth and poverty; where all are on the level of mere subsistence, the one is more able to give up his little to the other. The end of the communal struggle is life itself, and a vision of glory opens in the squalor of the moment, a vision that lifts up the minds of the deprived ones to a shared heaven in eternity. Heaven, whether in this world or the next, is an atmosphere of intimate fellowship with our neighbours, so that we know them as we are known by them. Possessions fall into the background, and such that there are become the property of all. The very thought of having something secret from another person is impossible. However, when the siege conditions of attrition are lifted, each person drifts along his own way, becomes imprisoned in his own private interests and shuts off from his awareness the concern for others that was once an essential part of his life. There is indeed a spark of God in the soul of each of us, but how easily it becomes obfuscated in the opacity of selfishness! The act of stealing concentrates that opaque darkness around the offender, remembering that the essence of theft is giving short measure of ourself in the various tests of life that confront us day by day. But when we know God in our lives, so often, as we have already noted on more than one occasion, when we are in a condition of extreme isolation, the light breaks into the darkness and we start to see clearly once more. 'All that came to be was alive with his life, and that life was the light of men. The light shines in the dark, and the darkness has never mastered it'

(John 1.4–5). As we know that light, so we give ourselves without reserve and cease to take anything that is not given to us in love. In the life of the world it is right that we should learn to conserve property. Private ownership is part of our training to become responsible, caring people. But as we grow in spiritual understanding, so our life-style becomes less complicated. Simplicity is an important fruit of the spiritual life, clouded by hardship and lightened by God's grace. There comes a time when we can understand quite directly Christ's severe strictures on wealth. 'How hard it is for the wealthy to enter the kingdom of God! It is easier for a camel to go through the eye of a needle than for a rich man to enter the kingdom of God' (Luke 18.24–5). It is not the wealth or possessions that are bad in themselves; what prevents their possessor from entering the Kingdom of God is their importance in his life. They, as idols, usurp the place of God and until they are given away for the common good and shed from the person of the rich man, they block his entry through the small gate and narrow road that leads to life, to quote from a collateral saying of Jesus (Matthew 7.13–14).

Much of this was witnessed in the lives of the early disciples. In the earliest community of all, those whose faith had drawn them together held everything in common; they would sell their property and possessions and make a general distribution as the need of each required (Acts 2.44–5). As the work progressed, so the members continued in this state of total sharing: not a man claimed any of his possessions as his own, but everything was held in common. They never had a needy person among them, because all who had property in land or houses sold it, brought the proceeds of the sale and laid the money at the feet of the apostles; it was then distributed to any who stood in need (Acts 4.32–5). Unfortunately this inspired communalism soon waned: whereas Barnabas sold his estate and gave over the money without demur, Ananias and Sapphira held back a part of the purchase-money of their property after having presented the remainder as the total price of the land. They lied to the Holy Spirit and were struck dead. However much we may shudder at the terrible fate meted out to the dishonest couple, it makes us realize even more forcibly what an unacceptable way of life is embraced in the act of stealing.

Only our best will do, whether in work for wages or in the unpaid service we afford in our personal relationships. When we withhold ourselves in the work of living, we are taking something precious without giving back full measure. The ideal society is that described in the early Acts of the Apostles where all the disciples held everything in common. But this state of affairs requires a complete change in heart of a community. It cannot be enforced by law; it can come only through love, which is God's supreme gift to us. The early disciples met that love in the incarnate and risen Christ. As he comes closer to us, so we will experience that love again, and then the divine community will appear, this time for ever.

9 ❧ The Inviolability of the Individual

'You shall not give false evidence against your neighbour' (Exodus 20.16).

We owe our fellow humans a great deal, because through them our lives attain balance and purpose. Martin Buber says that all real living is meeting. The variety of life in its constant parade brings forth variety of response in us also, an interminable stream of emotions and thoughts that fertilize our daily life and lay bare unimagined depths in the soul. Beneath the surface of even the most unprepossessing person there may lie worlds of fantasy and an urge towards fulfilment of immense creative possibilities. In this way meeting with other people exposes our own depths so that we begin to function as real people ourselves.

How do we come to know a person? An introduction followed by a polite conversation embracing topics of interest to us both may oil the wheels of social intercourse, but only the surfaces of the personalities are exposed in this transaction. For many people this degree of mutual sharing is quite enough; they have no desire to explore their own depths, let alone confront the emotional turbulence of the other person. Some of us are by nature inquisitive, trying to lay bare the very lives of all the throng we daily meet. In this way we can learn much of the life-history of the people, and yet we may remain as far from their true identity as when we first met them. We can know much about others by painstaking inquiry, but we cannot know a person in this way. Indeed, it is hard, if not impossible, to know anyone by a direct personal onslaught. The one assailed in this way will retreat summarily into his shell of reticence, avoiding further contact, or else he will open up with a variable repartee of falsehood mixed with wishful thinking, hoping to impress his interrogator.

It is actually easier to know God than either oneself or some other person. The reason for this paradoxical state of affairs – remembering that no one can see or delineate the Almighty – is that God is freely available to us in the depth of our own being when we are quiet enough to attend to the moment in hand. While we can never come to him on our own terms, he is eternally at hand to meet us, and he accepts us for ourselves alone. He has no favourites nor does he reject even the mightiest sinner – who is potentially any one of us at a particular time. Once we know the unlimited acceptance of God in the depths of the soul, we can begin to accept ourselves without the need for either justification or propitiatory mortification. At last we can breathe in the power of the Holy Spirit, and a new life opens for us. This is one application of the teaching of John 3.3; unless a man has been born over again, he cannot see the Kingdom of God. The sacrament of baptism is the outer sign of this new birth, but in due course it is experienced in the soul's centre, or spirit, in a personal encounter with God.

As we breathe in the power of the Holy Spirit, so we are transformed personally. As we undergo personal transformation, so the power of the Holy Spirit radiates from us to all those around us – and at a distance in the prayer of intercession. Now at last we can effect a deep, caring relationship with other people, both individually and collectively. We do not need to strive to know people by displaying our gifts and social eligibility. Instead, we can remain completely still and at peace within, while a stream of love so pours down from us that we are in the most intimate fellowship even with complete strangers. True personal knowledge is a state of union with the other; indeed, unitive knowledge is the apogee of all understanding. In this knowledge the two, while retaining their unique identities, are now functionally one, and there follows an unembarrassed sharing of inner problems, tensions and fears. There is also an unlimited flow of spiritual strength from the one to the other, and with this there comes an undisturbed trust and a warmth of love that far exceeds any superficial affection that we may experience on a purely social level.

When we know this degree of spiritual intimacy with another person, we are inevitably in close fellowship with many other people also, for with the breaking down of our own barriers, we are fully available to the world while remaining rooted in our own unique nature. In this state of open friendship it would be impossible to betray anyone, let alone give false evidence against him. On the contrary, as the barriers of the personality drop from us, so we can rejoice in the splendid uniqueness of each fellow being while participating with delight in that special gift. Thus we acknowledge and support the individual nature of each person we encounter in a day's work. It is indeed a social duty to uphold our fellow creatures, supporting their legitimate endeavours and protecting them against injury and injustice. But what starts as a law of social action becomes a passionate response from the soul as we live in the depths of our fellow men.

To undermine a neighbour is tantamount to destroying him. The sin of bearing false witness, or giving untrue evidence, threatens his reputation, challenges his personal authority, puts his livelihood in jeopardy and may easily end his life. It can be linked to the sin of making wrong use of God's name, when that name is invoked to swear falsely against another person. Perjury is the extreme use of evil communication to destroy another person's life. It is the ultimate sin against God himself, putting his name at the disposal of the evil forces that so often appear to be in control of the world. Usually the attack made on the name and character of a fellow human being is less dramatic than this. It more often involves the use of subtle innuendo veiled by ingenious half-truth to cast a smear on his integrity. In this way a person's career can be blighted and a promising relationship between two people wrecked. The tendency towards calumny is one of the commonest sins in everyday life, so much so that when we encounter a genuinely kindly person who bears no rancour against his neighbour and refuses to add his quota to a general foray against an absent member by the assembled mass, we are immediately arrested in our tracks. Sometimes, of course, the uncritical person is merely simplistic in his approach to his fellows, remaining blissfully unperceptive of their baser motives. But on other occasions, the kindly one is a very evolved person on the spiritual level, one who has traversed many hardships himself and has learned a greater charity as a result of his own humiliation. Charity follows the chequered experience of life, and is more developed in the later stages of our career on earth. It is quite a different quality to permissiveness, which is negligent and detached. Charity is in essence a mature, wise distillation of love and experience, caring and committed, seeking to preserve the evil-doer for the good that is within him also. An emotionally mature person is, as we have already noted in connection with sexual relationships, an exceptional phenomenon; he takes no pleasure in gossip and scandal, preferring to regard his fellows kindly and to keep his own counsel.

Why, in fact, do we tend to speak ill of our neighbours? Why in daily living do we so often flinch from the truth, and utter falsehoods? In some instances there is a deep-seated hatred against a particular national, racial or religious group to which the victim belongs, and in others there is an unfortunate association between a particularly invidious situation in the past and the present circumstance to which the victim relates. In these respects we can recall with horror the enormous calumnies directed against the Jews in past ages as well as in our own century. They have been accused by their detractors not only of plotting world domination but also of indulging in foul ritual practices using infants' blood. The result of the hatred based on jealousy and inflamed by the fear that ignorance engenders was the mass persecution of Jews in European pogroms down many centuries and the wholesale murders of the Nazi era. It was said by the minister of propaganda of the Nazi régime that the greater the lie, the more likely was it to be believed. Another vile persecution, this time of Catholics, took place in England in the latter part of the seventeenth century, following the publicizing of the false popish plot by Titus Oates and his associates. These terrible instances of mass persecution and indiscriminate killing following the spread of false evidence against innocent groups of people reveal how near the surface of the personality of most of us are cesspits of hatred against our fellow creatures. When all is going smoothly for us we can afford to display our tolerance, even concern, for the stranger in our midst. But once we are threatened with financial loss, we soon reveal a baser side to our character. To retain our supremacy and that of our family (the 'little tiger' of William Morris) we will all too often stoop to the vilest calumnies against the foreigner or the individual who is somewhat isolated because of an unorthodox style of life.

One of the most unseemly aspects of hatred against racial and religious groups is the tendency for the individual victim to become totally submerged in the hated group. Those who hate such groups are in fact creating scapegoats whom they can subsequently attack and destroy in bulk. The individual member of the proscribed group loses his precious identity, at least in the eyes of his detractors, and becomes a representative worthy only of ostracism and destruction. This process of degrading the person by lowering him to the common herd is diametrically opposed to the love we should bear another person in the light of God's universal love, when he ceases to be a mere member of the crowd and becomes an individual of value in his own right. The executive power of evil strives continually to destroy all that is noble and good, bringing the creatures down as a mass to the primal chaos from which they originally emerged by the divine word and act. The way of Christ, by contrast, lifts prostitutes, tax-gatherers and other sinners to the height of their unique promise, so that they begin to shed the old ways and enter a new life of purpose, sacrifice and transfiguration. In this respect it is as ill-conceived to favour certain groups unduly as it is to denigrate them. Whereas the race-hater herds together all individuals who bear the proscribed name irrespective of their moral stature and longs, at least unconsciously, for their exposure and final destruction, the race-lover places all members of the favoured group on a uniformly high pedestal of esteem, despite the obvious unworthiness of some individuals. The error of esteeming national or religious groups on a personal level is as fundamental as that of denigrating them *en masse*: an ideology takes the place of a living relationship, and the individual members of the group become mere pawns in the mind of the idealist. They cease to be real people who can be met in a living situation and whose witness can enrich society as a whole.

Jealousy is probably the most important factor leading us to give false evidence against a neighbour. What we ourselves have failed to achieve we begrudge in the life of someone more favoured than we are. That we may in fact be less worthy than the other person is too intolerable to consider, and instead we conjure up fantasies of intrigue and subversion to explain how others always fare better than we do. That underhand manipulations do sometimes allow less worthy contenders to win the accolade of public esteem is well known. That secret cabals may play a part in misdirecting justice is no idle thought, but in the end those who work subversively earn their reward of exposure and humiliation. People attaining spiritual mastery do not patronize these circles. The false accusations levelled at Christ were an amalgam of jealousy and fear. His opponents could not bear his effortless spiritual superiority and they were afraid that he would expose their weakness to the crowds. In fact, had they trusted Jesus, he would have supported their frailty and given them strength to face the darkness within them. But pride prevented them from either opening themselves to him or permitting his healing love to suffuse their distorted personalities with new life. Pride is certainly the deadliest of the sins because it will neither yield itself nor receive love from anyone else. Therefore it leads to absolute stagnation, until its proverbial departure before the inevitable fall: only a major calamity can force it to be relinquished, and then at last the power of love can penetrate the bereft personality. Rancour, jealousy and the fear of being exposed in one's naked impotence all feed pride, which in turn will plot to put an end to anyone who may threaten its tenuous security.

We may also be tempted to give false evidence against a fellow creature because of fear, itself often a product of ignorance. Throughout the earlier centuries of our era there was a fear of witchcraft, so that any person suspected of possessing unusual psychic faculties was in great danger of denunciation and death. Most of the victims of this calumny were women, who are in any case generally more sensitive psychically and more aware intuitively than men. These tend to function most efficiently physically and intellectually; in this way the sexes complement each other. Quite a number of women denounced as witches were either victims of deliberate malice or else somewhat disturbed mentally; in those days, mental illness was regarded as a demonic manifestation and the insane were treated with great cruelty. We can give thanks that the modern scientific age has put an end to much subterranean denunciation of innocent people on charges of witchcraft, as knowledge of the workings of the mind has replaced primitive superstition. On the other hand, the modern mind is not the measure of all things. The unconscious is the repository of psychic powers that transcend purely rational understanding, and these are our way of knowing both the spiritual realm and its demonic counterpart.

The fact of evil must neither be allowed undue domination nor should it be smoothly eased out of our awareness by plausible rationalizations. In our own psyche and the collective unconscious of mankind there are dark, subterranean elements of great potency that could do untold harm if ignored, for then they would be given free rein. That some psychically attuned people work in concert with demonic agencies is as certain as that others work with the communion of saints and the ministry of angels. Those whose allegiance is to the demonic are practitioners of witchcraft and their influence should not be disregarded. But they are not to be persecuted, let alone destroyed. Their actions will be their own condemnation, and eventually they will crawl for assistance to those who are able to help them by the grace of God. The right way to counter this menace is by informed education on psychical matters, religious observance and especially the practice of constant prayer. In the intangible, nebulous psychic realms it is the power of God that alone can cleanse a contaminated atmosphere; we assist the Deity best by contemplative prayer and faithful intercession for those who are in special danger. When we plot against those whom we suspect of evil in these realms we play into the hands of the forces of darkness. In the words of Christ, 'Love your enemies, and pray for your persecutors; only so can you be children of your heavenly Father' (Matthew 5.44–5). St Paul expands on this theme in Romans 12.17–20, when he instructs us never to pay back evil for evil, and to let our aims be such as all men count honourable. If humanly possible we should live at peace with everyone. Above all, we should not seek revenge, but leave a place for divine retribution. We should not let evil conquer us, but use good to defeat evil. It can, in other words, never be right to give false evidence to convict even a person of known criminal associations whom one would wish to eliminate entirely from the society of innocent people. The end does not justify the means.

We can also be tempted to give false evidence in order to curry favour with those in authority, or to gain the approval of those whose influence we might later use for our own ends. Thus Jezebel arranged for two scoundrels to charge Naboth with cursing God and the king: Naboth was sentenced to death by stoning, and Ahab went to take possession of his vineyard (1 Kings 21). However, the wrath of God, which is the full working of his law of cause and effect, descended on Ahab and Jezebel, and both died appalling deaths. In the instance of Jesus, it was Judas Iscariot who betrayed him by an allegation that remains obscure. In the subsequent trial, many came forward with false evidence but little of it tallied. He was accused of claiming to pull down the temple of God and then rebuild it in three days, to which he kept silence. A not very dissimilar accusation was levelled at Stephen before his martyrdom, when false witnesses were produced to claim that he was continually saying things against the temple and the Law, and that Jesus himself would destroy the temple and alter the customs handed down by Moses (Acts 6.11–14). When men of noble character fall foul of popular approval there is no end of calumny that will be flung against them. Indeed, there are few more enjoyable experiences for unregenerate people than to witness the humiliation of the righteous. Those who stood in amused approval as Christ hung from the cross have taken their places in the mobs that hounded unpopular minority groups to death in later centuries. Christ himself always takes his place with the persecuted, for he knows what terror enters the hearts of those about to be killed with wanton brutality. He would also take his place with the persecutors, for he understands the warped minds of those who can only destroy that which is beyond their comprehension. But they must know themselves in truth before they can accept Christ among them.

In the far less dramatic environment of everyday life we stab the reputations of the people close to us and of whom we are unconsciously jealous, especially when we are bored and dispirited. Character assassination comes easily to those whose minds have no creative work to plan. It is well said that the devil always finds work for idle hands to do; how much more potent is the mischief sown by the mouth of one whose mind is empty and whose life has no overall purpose! Mischief-making is a common and very destructive social evil. It trades on the weaknesses that we all inherit, and inflates a minor indiscretion into the stature of a major misdemeanour so that the unfortunate victim is placed subtly but irrevocably outside the pale of the society of his peers. No longer can he be trusted, as his presence becomes increasingly offensive to those who at one time counted him a valuable colleague. Personal friendships of long-standing have been destroyed by mean-hearted scandalmongers who have sown distrust and aversion where once there was warm affection. Shakespeare portrayed this catastrophic sequence in the innocent love between Othello and Desdemona subtly undermined by the calculated insinuations of Iago, who is a symbol of the devil wrecking human relationships and bringing all fellowship to the chaos of distrust, loathing and murder.

When we consider the sorry situation of evidence falsely given against a fellow human, we are brought up sharply against the divided attitudes we ourselves all too often exhibit towards those around us. Even those whom we sincerely admire we secretly envy. Those whom we believe we love we often distrust inwardly. When someone whom we have genuinely esteemed is discountenanced, possibly unjustly, how often do we secretly exult in his humiliation while publicly proclaiming our shock and indignation, rather like Job's comforters! Betrayal is a constant human theme. Indeed, it is probably necessary for all of us to experience its bitter ache, for it cuts us down to size, the size of a little child. Human awareness expands more through the darkness of isolation born of suffering than in the garish glow of hearty conviviality. The uncomfortable lesson that we all have our price and no one can be totally relied on causes us to turn our trust to the One who alone does not fail us. When we know God we no longer require the support of human solidarity, and then, paradoxically, a tenderness is born in us that can take in and accept all human frailty. As we have faced our own vulnerability, so we can protect all that is vulnerable in other people. Love blossoms authentically when we know we have nothing to offer except ourselves in our tragic weakness. It may be that Jesus himself gained the final victory of the spirit when he gave up his own tortured spirit to his Father, and he left the world that had so shabbily received his service with pure forgiveness.

It is in the spirit of forgiveness that we cease to think evil of other people. When we are bereft of all selfish ambition and can be open to the present moment in joyful acceptance, we are also receptive to all life. We can accept everything as it stands without judgement, indeed with thanksgiving that we have been chosen to participate in the world's history at this present time and in this particular situation. It is when the mind is not focused in one-pointed awareness on the matter at hand that it starts to drift aimlessly into realms that are not productive. Among these unhelpful domains are the affairs of other people. Vain imagining leads to false judgements and jealousy, and soon the mind has conjured up a series of potential enemies who must, from that time onwards, be carefully watched lest they cause one harm. Therefore when Jesus says, 'Pass no judgement, and you will not be judged. For as you judge others, so you will yourselves be judged, and whatever measure you deal out to others will be dealt back to you' (Matthew 7.1-2), he is stating a fundamental law of life. As we colour life with our own opinions and distort it with our prejudices, so these aberrations return to us as surely as the waves of the sea beat against the shore according to the tide. A great advance in our understanding breaks through when we learn to accept people with joy on the particular rung of the ladder of spiritual growth that they have attained. Then we need no longer make unnecessary demands on those of modest understanding any more than envy those far advanced on the spiritual path.

It is when we are deeply centred in the soul that we are centred in humanity also. God is known in the highest point of the soul, and he is the integrating factor in all our relationships. His Spirit leads us all on to our final encounter with reality whose human form is Christ. To sum up the whole matter: if we are to speak the truth about our neighbour, we must be centred in the truth about ourselves, and this truth is that God is nearer to us than our own being when we are still and aware of the present moment. St Paul puts it thus: 'The secret is this: Christ in you, the hope of a glory to come' (Colossians 1.27). This Christ is also among us in the divine community of which we are an integral part. When we know this with our heart, soul and mind, we will fulfil the injunction 'This is what you shall do: speak the truth to each other, administer true and sound judgement in the city gate. Do not contrive any evil one against another, and do not love perjury, for all this I hate' (Zechariah 8.16–17). When the love of God reigns in our heart we will never again imagine evil against any person.

10 ❧ The Transmutation of Desire

'You shall not covet your neighbour's house; you shall not covet your neighbour's wife, his slave, his slave-girl, his ox, his ass or anything that belongs to him' (Exodus 20.17).

Desire is the emotional stimulus that sets in action all purposeful activity. Hunger and thirst stimulate the body to search for sustenance that will assuage their pangs. Likewise, sexual desire finds its fulfilment in copulation which may end in the conception of a new individual. Without desire nothing would be achieved; we would live in an inanimate world not so much dead as never having been alive. However, if desire is the power behind the onward movement of life, it is also the cause of suffering. The great religions of the East, especially Buddhism, stress the connection between the suffering that is an aspect of mortal life and human desire. Only when we have moved beyond desire can there be an end of suffering, and for this purpose an enlightened way of life is prescribed. The Noble Eightfold Path of Buddhism shares points in common with the Ten Commandments; the purpose of both great doctrines of the good life is a raising of the selfish consciousness of the unenlightened person to a dimension that transcends the ego and embraces the whole community, finding its summation in the realm of the divine. We remember in passing that the Buddhist way has no use for a personal God, but is concerned rather with the eternal law of life, the dharma (or dhamma in the Pali script). The dharma can be equated with the eternal uncreated consciousness from which all creation proceeds and which penetrates, informs and judges every action of life whether in this world or in the realms beyond death. When we co-operate with the universal law of the dharma, our personal desires merge and dissolve into a reality that transcends all discursive thought, and we enter the formless, transpersonal consciousness of nirvana (or nibbana).

While this may indeed be the ultimate truth, there is no doubt that desire plays an essential part in our earthly existence. Jesus himself said, 'How have I longed to eat this Passover with you before my death. For I tell you, never again shall I eat it until the time when it finds its fulfilment in the Kingdom of God' (Luke 22.15–16). With loving desire he had waited to share this last meal with his disciples, so that they could proceed to celebrate his sacramental giving of himself to them and to all the world after he had left them. We too celebrate the sacrament of the Eucharist until he comes to share it with us in the Kingdom of God, when all earthly things are changed into spiritual radiance. Desire impels us onwards to our next work; according to the nature of that desire, the action performed is either good or bad, but without desire there would be no development in our lives, and the world would founder in stagnation and death. It is evident that there are two levels of desire, one that has to be outgrown if we are to become truly adult and mature in our humanity, and the other that has to be obeyed if we are to attain fulfilment as spiritual beings.

Covetousness represents essentially the lower level of desire. It craves eagerly, almost insatiably, for that which belongs to another person, and to attain its end it would quite happily resort to evil actions, for it cannot rest until it has gained possession of what it desires. It is grasping, its nature is avarice, and it dominates the thoughts of the person who suffers under it. Stealing, giving false evidence, and murder are all potential fruits of a covetous nature. So also is adultery when the covetousness is tinged with lust. In the biblical narrative covetousness is a recurring theme. Jacob coveted Esau's birthright which was his brother's due as the elder of the twins, and he acquired it under duress when his brother was exhausted and famished. Later he was to gain his father Isaac's blessing by impersonating Esau, whom his blind father preferred to Jacob. Jacob's covetousness cost him Esau's friendship, and he had to flee to escape his brother's murderous intentions. Nevertheless, in this primitive story, whose morality was still undeveloped as compared with the later teachings of the Law and the prophets, Jacob's unscrupulous actions seem to have been justified inasmuch as he was far more worthy than his coarse, sensual brother to fulfil the divine plan for Israel's election.

In the later scriptural narrative, covetousness is more clearly sinful. An especially despicable instance mars the life story of David, who covets the wife of Uriah the Hittite, a humble soldier in David's service and a man of greater morality than his royal master. Having seduced Bathsheba, David plots the death of Uriah at the battle front, after which he takes Uriah's widow as his own (2 Samuel 11). Thus the act of covetousness culminates in the murder of an innocent, noble man, but it sets in action a sequence of disasters in David's own family, culminating in his favourite son Absalom rising in mutiny against him. The nation is divided, and although Absalom's insurrection fails and he himself is killed in battle, David is heartbroken at the death of his son. His initial act of lustful desire had set in motion fateful repercussions within his own family, ending in his own fight for survival and the death of his beloved son, now become his mortal enemy.

Another fearful episode of covetousness concerns Ahab and his desire to possess the vineyard of Naboth. When Naboth refuses to hand over this family land to the king, Ahab, acting through the perfidy of his wife Jezebel, has Naboth falsely accused of cursing God and the king. Once Naboth has been stoned to death for alleged blasphemy and disloyalty, Ahab sallies forth to take possession of the property. But God, through the prophet Elijah, denounces the royal couple, forecasting disaster for them and a complete wiping out of the family line (1 Kings 21), events that occupy the end of the first Book of Kings and the beginning of the second Book. Thus the covetousness of David and Ahab led to the callous murder of their respective victims, but the destruction they executed was visited upon them much magnified. David, however, was truly penitent, and led a more upright life after the sequence of family tragedies, whereas Ahab was basically evil and moved inexorably towards the annihilation of his dynasty.

In the New Testament narrative, covetousness once again rears its head, this time in connection with spiritual gifts rather than material wealth or sexual lust. The most notorious account concerns the magician Simon who was active in Samaria. The charismatic gifts of Philip the deacon impressed him sufficiently to accept baptism, but his cupidity was stimulated almost to the point of explosion when the apostles Peter and John appeared on the scene: when they prayed over the converts with the laying-on of hands, they bestowed the Holy Spirit on them. Simon offered them money, to acquire the same power of bestowing the Spirit. Peter denounced him forthwith, forecasting a bitter future for him unless he repented of his wickedness, for Simon was fundamentally dishonest with God (Acts 8.9–24). The sin of simony, the buying or selling of ecclesiastical preferment, takes its name from this episode in the life of the early Church.

God's gift is not to be coveted. It comes by grace to those who are empty of selfishness, not to those who would use it for their own benefit. Indeed, even those who do receive the gifts of the Holy Spirit have to be inwardly cleansed of personal impurities before they can become worthy ministers of God, and the process of purgation goes on ceaselessly throughout their life on earth and, no doubt, in the life beyond death also. Likewise, the spiritual gifts that are used to succour those in need bear no charge. The gift is its own reward for the one possessing it, and the joy of being able to assist a person in distress is the greatest recompense anyone could desire. Once we use the gifts of God to inflate our own personalities or to strengthen our position in the society in which we work, these blessings assume a demonic power. Thus we read Jesus' stark warning:

> Not everyone who calls me 'Lord, Lord' will enter the kingdom of heaven, but only those who do the will of my heavenly Father. When that day comes, many will say to me, 'Lord, Lord, did we not prophesy in your name, cast out devils in your name, and in your name perform many miracles?' Then I will tell them to their face, 'I never knew you; out of my sight, you and your wicked ways' (Matthew 7.21–3).

We are brought once again to the fundamental spiritual teaching about the eternal life of the true self as opposed to the flickering existence of the ego consciousness. It is the staple of all the world's great mystical traditions, and is expressed particularly cogently in the gospel:

> Then he called the people to him, as well as his disciples, and said to them, 'Anyone who wishes to be a follower of mine must leave self behind; he must take up his cross, and come with me. Whoever cares for his own safety is lost; but if a man will let himself be lost for my sake and for the gospel, that man is safe. What does a man gain by winning the whole world at the cost of his true self? What can he give to buy that self back?' (Mark 8.34–7).

The self that has to be left behind is the ego that demands rights and privileges for itself. What it lacks it will seek covetously in the other person, but it will never be satisfied. The riches of this world are mere illusions if substantial support or protection is expected from them. The more we have, the more we covet, and yet our basic insecurity remains unhealed. Possessions, whether of things or people, never really belong to us, for we can be stripped of them overnight. Indeed, only when we have taken up our cross and left the ego image behind can we pursue the great work of following our Lord. This cross represents the particular defect we have to bear in our incarnation: it may be a tendency to ill-health, a moral weakness, a mental instability, a difficulty of temperament or a social incubus. The heart knows its own bitterness, and a stranger has no part in its joy (Proverbs 14.10). The cross may be temporarily concealed during the day's delights, but when the evening comes it is stripped for all the world to see. And then the world sees Jesus nailed to the cross once more. This is our final test, and if we cling to God alone, we too will pass from death to immortality, from the crucifixion of mortal life to the resurrection of eternity.

Thus the person who cares for his own safety – in other words his mortal life to the exclusion of all else – is lost, for all the rewards of this world are necessarily consummated in mortality; not one can be taken with us when we die. On the other hand, when we have sacrificed all we have and are for God, as revealed in Christ, the immortal principle of the spirit is revealed in us. This is eternal and of the nature of Christ. What indeed are all the world's riches in comparison with the immortal self that is the repository and guardian of the moral values to which all true religion bears witness? Whatever we covet we put in the place of that spark of God which is the light of men, a light that issues from the eternal life of the Word, from whom all life proceeds, to quote from the prologue of the fourth Gospel. Thus a covetous nature obscures the light of God that burns in the spirit of the soul, until the divine flame is occluded by worldly encumbrances.

It was the tragedy of the rich young man who came to Christ for instructions about the attainment of eternal life to be so encumbered with the riches of this world that he was unable to let them go. If only he had had the courage to make this final renunciation, his soul would have shone forth with the radiance of the spirit within, and he would have attained a knowledge of eternity there and then. As we have more than once stressed, it is neither the ego nor the things of this world that are bad – in fact, they are all essential for our well-being while we are alive in the world. What makes them dangerous is our tendency to cling to them. Personal craving and covetous desire pervert all the beautiful things of life, including the most intimate personal relationships. But when all is given to God and the service of our fellow men, we are not only free of a mounting incubus, but are also given back what we renounced, a thousand times glorified. Our own needs are fully satisfied, and now we can work towards the satisfaction of the needs of all other people instead of being imprisoned in our own insecurity, which in turn nourishes a covetous attitude to life.

The only possession we can take for granted in this strange life is our own being, and how little do we know of its intricacies! We are a motley collection, an assemblage, of gifts and defects housed in an indifferent body. Our great work in life is to integrate the various facets of our complex personality into an efficient working unit, so that what was previously divided and at war within us can now be united, accepted, healed and blessed by the power of God. The power, the Holy Spirit, is always available, but he cannot act until we have attained sufficient awareness to call upon God for help. This is essentially the nature of petitionary prayer. By contrast, there is a perverse way of seeking inner healing, and this involves the coveting of qualities and possessions from outside ourselves. Whatever we covet serves in essence to plaster over a crack in our personality, concealing our incompleteness from the outside world (and all too often from our own inner scrutiny as well). Thus we live as blurred, unreal people.

The person who is inwardly insecure may, for instance, plausibly ascribe his feelings of unease to financial stress or social inferiority. He may unconsciously be driven by this insecurity to devote his life to acquiring money or attaining status in his social or professional milieu. And yet while an impressive façade of dross is being erected on the surface of the personality, there lies beneath it the wounded heart of a little child, seeking pitifully for acknowledgement and love. It is indeed ironical that the more such a deprived person attains by coveting the world, the further does he distance himself from any truly living relationship and therefore from any possibility of love. Thus the great social evils denounced in the Ten Commandments stem ultimately from inner incompleteness: we are tempted to kill, steal, lie and covet in order to protect ourselves from the frank admission of our own intrinsic deficiency. What we lack in ourselves we will grasp surreptitiously from our neighbour even if this involves his injury to the point of death.

Fortunately, the inner defect that has been plastered over in this way will in due course split open to public view as our moral bankruptcy becomes obvious to everyone. The sooner we are exposed, the more fortunate it is for us because the ensuing humiliation, severe punishment as it is, is the first step in our rehabilitation. Exposure and ostracism bring the offender rapidly to his senses, so that he can at last face the corruption within himself, confess his sins and await forgiveness. Forgiveness is the essential therapy in the healing of all delinquencies: 'For all alike have sinned and are deprived of the divine splendour, and all are justified by God's free grace alone' (Romans 3.24). As the offender seeks forgiveness, so the social background that led to his covetous inclinations is exposed, and this too has to be forgiven in retrospect, for no good comes from the constant bearing of a grudge. Thus do we pray that God will forgive us our sins as we are empowered by him to forgive those who sin against us. Indeed, all sin forms part of a continuum of perverse action.

As we receive forgiveness, so may love slowly enter our hearts while an understanding of the frailties of other people is granted us. He who has not traversed his own dark pit of suffering and faced exposure to the truth of his situation can seldom feel compassion for his erring neighbour. Empathy comes most easily to those who have attained self-knowledge in dereliction; when we are no longer chained to diverting delusions of self-importance, we become free enough of self-absorption to admit other people into our private lives. On coming to know them better, we can begin to accept ourselves as we are with a fresh thanksgiving that does not depend on veiled comparisons with other people. In this way we attain a genuine self-esteem that is based on the amazed recognition of our uniqueness, but is not tied to personal gifts or triumphs in daily life. When we can hold our head high in affirming our own splendid identity, we can affirm with equal delight the identity of all around us, needing neither to denigrate them nor exalt them on a pedestal of special esteem. In this way the tendency towards coveting anything from anyone finally leaves us.

It is important to realize that while an amelioration of adverse social conditions is important in providing the basic needs of life, these alone, even in profusion, will not put an end to the tendency to covet, steal, lie or murder. The core of sinful action lies deep within the soul; in theological terms it is called original sin, and it seems to be an inevitable by-product, almost a concomitant, of the free will the Creator has bestowed on his rational creatures. We, as human beings, are given a freedom of choice, the means of a free, unobstructed movement towards self-actualization. If we use God's gift of will wisely we tend towards the good life, but even then the full understanding of what that goodness entails comes slowly to us through life's many experiences, some joyful and others tragic. When at last, perhaps after an experience comparable with that of the prodigal son sitting in destitution among the pigs, we grasp the primary truth of the spiritual life that our greatest personal good brings with it a corresponding benefit to our fellow creatures also, we are moving from the world of covetousness to that of sacrifice. This is the way shown by Christ, who gave of his riches to his brothers: he became poor so that they might be rich. But his poverty embraces all riches, transfiguring them from inert articles of worldly splendour to sacraments of the risen life.

The tragedies of life expose a void in the soul that the person all too readily seeks to fill with attributes taken from the common stockpile. Eventually by bitter experience he has to learn that the repair can proceed only from the elements of his own personality. Only then will he be filled with something that will never be taken away, but will instead grow to profusion. When Jesus expounded the mystery of the Holy Spirit to the Samaritan woman, he showed the way to a spiritual outpouring that can have no end. 'Everyone who drinks this water will be thirsty again, but whoever drinks the water that I shall give him will never suffer thirst any more. The water that I shall give him will be an inner spring always welling up for eternal life' (John 4.14).

The craving for personal belongings and attributes is therefore part of our childhood. It provides us with a sense of security, permitting us to hold our head high in the company of our peers. In the same way the exhibition of professional qualifications confirms the status of the inexperienced graduate. But all this can act merely as an impressive smoke-screen concealing the identity of the person behind a façade of pomp and grandeur. It may well have to be dissipated before the inner validity of the person is revealed: it is what we are that alone matters in a time of crisis, for neither possessions nor academic honours can help us effectively then. The reputation we may have built up previously in terms of popular acclaim is tested in the crucible of suffering, and what emerges from the fire of attrition is our authentic nature. Jesus came through his ordeal entire and glorified; Peter, so sure of his absolute loyalty to Christ, emerged after his third denial of ever having known the Lord shattered and in tears. His glib assurance and ambivalent loyalty lay incinerated; all that remained was a scorched heart palpitating with shame. When their master was alive, the disciples coveted the best places at the heavenly banquet presided over by Christ himself. When they came to themselves, after the death and resurrection of Christ and the downflow of the Holy Spirit upon them, they were to give up their lives for the conversion of the world to their risen master, remembering his words that the true master is the servant of all.

As we grow in spiritual stature, so we crave for the healing of the world. Our own life assumes importance inasmuch as it can be used to God's honour and glory. The desire that once was directed to our own interests is now extended to the welfare of our neighbour, who finally includes every member of the human family – and from that family to every living creature in the world. Reverence for life finds its completion in the resurrection of the entire created universe, so that everything is brought back to the Father in spiritual radiance. In this way desire is transfigured as covetousness drops away and a burning concern for all created things occupies our thoughts and actions.

Should we therefore be concerned about ourselves at all? The answer is given categorically in that part of the Sermon on the Mount dealing with detachment (Matthew 6.25–34), in which Jesus admonishes us to put away anxious thoughts about food and drink to keep us alive, and clothes to cover our body. This is not because they are unimportant but because God already knows our need. What we have to do is to set our mind on God's Kingdom and his justice before everything else, and all the rest will come to us as well. Once we have lifted up our minds to God in prayer, his spirit so infuses us that our daily work is conducted with efficiency and in harmony with those around us. We cease to covet that which does not belong to us, and instead work with concentrated application in the present moment. Desire indeed drops away from us, ceasing to be the stimulus for further activity, and we are now perfectly aligned to the divine will. Thus the two perfect prayers are those of Mary at the time of the annunciation – 'As you have spoken, so be it' (Luke 1.38) – and of her son in agony at Gethsemane – 'Father, if it be thy will, take this cup from me. Yet not my will, but thine be done' (Luke 22.42). When we desire to do God's will and wait patiently in the work of the present moment for this to be revealed to us, we move beyond personal desire to perfect service. And then we know a freedom of action that comes from God alone, for we no longer have to please men in order to gain their approval.

Even a desire to help others, laudable as it may appear on the surface, may carry with it unconscious elements of domination. Only when we are centred fully in God can our actions be harmless. As St Paul puts it, 'I have been crucified with Christ:

the life I now live is not my life, but the life which Christ lives in me' (Galatians 2.19). Once the lower nature has been crucified and therefore ceases to make inordinate demands on the environment, a higher power within us can take charge. This is the spiritual self concentrated in the soul and issuing from the spirit. Christ lives in the spirit of each of us, and when he is fully operative in our lives we cease to demand anything – even the well-being of our neighbour. Instead we can give of ourself humbly to his service and confidently leave the final outcome of the transaction to God alone. Equanimity replaces both personal covetousness and a passionate concern for the rights of others that all too often explodes in violence and hatred. Whatever we desire for others, no matter how commendable it may appear, is coloured by our own prejudices and shortcomings. When we are centred in God in contemplative prayer, our own desires melt away, except for the supreme desire of doing God's will. At that point we move from circumscribed personal existence to the shared life of eternity where God, ourself and our neighbour are all one. Personal desire has been transfigured to service for all life, and what comes from us has a healing power beyond all rational understanding.

In a wonderful way the final commandment brings us back once more to the first: you shall have no other god to set against me. When we worship God in spirit and truth, we have attained all that life can give us. There is nothing left that could be coveted, for we are filled with the divine grace compared with which all material wealth, all intellectual brilliance and all social grandeur are as nothing. Desire has been transcended, except the ceaseless ache in the heart that all people may know the truth that sets them free from material illusion so that they too may share in the life of eternity.

11 ✑ The Summing Up

> *'Then one of the lawyers, who had been listening to*
> *these discussions and had noted how well he*
> *answered, came forward and asked him, "Which*
> *commandment is first of all?" Jesus answered, "The*
> *first is, Hear, O Israel: the Lord our God is the only*
> *Lord; love the Lord your God with all your heart,*
> *with all your soul, with all your mind, and with all*
> *your strength." The second is this: "Love your*
> *neighbour as yourself." There is no other*
> *commandment greater than these'* (Mark 12.28–31).

The summing up of the law of God is love, as St Paul writes
in Romans 13.10. When we know the full impact of love it
is impossible to do wrong to our neighbour. We have already
traced the process by which we know the love that transforms
our lives. Love comes from God, and we love because of that
divine love coming to us, not because we deserve it but because
it is God's nature to have love for all his creatures. We are all
too often closed to the power of God's love because of the
diversions of the world, but when human support fails and we
are left to fare for ourself, we become open to God's presence
and can accept his unconditional love. Then for the first time
in our life we are able to accept ourself as we are, no longer
having to hide our defects or to protect ourself against the
scrutiny of others by erecting an imposing superstructure around
ourself. As we begin to accept ourself in this way, so we are
able to accept other people with equal freedom. We can enter
into their lives, feel into their personalities and share their
woes and delights. This empathy may attain a mystical quality
when we can affirm a shared identity with all that lives. Then
anything that wounds another person hurts us with an equal
intensity. It is in this spirit that we arrive at the golden rule:
always treat others as you would like them to treat you, for this
is the Law and the prophets (Matthew 7.12). This rule attains
fulfilment only as we have acquired sufficient self-control to
be constantly aware of our own reactions to the various events
of life and the deepening knowledge of the self that accrues
from that awareness. At the same time our growing empathy

with all life allows us to project that awareness on to those around us. In this frame of mind it is impossible to do anyone else a wrong, for in so doing we injure ourselves equally.

Love therefore comprises three actions: an openness to God's eternal providence, an acceptance of ourself in our present situation with an equally full acceptance of our neighbour, and a free self-giving to our neighbour that he may attain the fullness of being God has in store for him. Expressed thus, loving sounds like unremitting hard work, and so it is. Love is an act of consecrated will whereby we offer ourself unconditionally for the healing of the world under the obedience of God's love to us as revealed by the Holy Spirit. In fact, when we act in love, God fills us with his love so that we grow in spiritual stature as we enable others to grow likewise. In other words, love is not merely an ecstatic emotional experience of fellowship without any explicit commitment to act. Neither is it a hard, joyless vigil of self-renunciation in which we give up everything for the sake of other people. This type of service is so bound up with ideals of duty and mortification that it does not in fact relate either to God or to our neighbour. Much traditional 'charity' had this unpleasant aura around it, so that it was proverbially described as cold. In the same way the traditional odour of sanctity often had the mustiness of a stuffy room about it rather than the fragrance of incense.

Love is not to be identified with affection. While affection is valuable in its own right, it cannot be relied on. It is here today and gone tomorrow, because though warm and embracing and full of goodwill, it is liable to wane disastrously as circumstances change. It depends for its ardour on the equable behaviour of the other person, and once he has let one's expectations falter, he is rapidly dropped from his seat of favour. It is not too uncommon to be summarily dismissed from the company of someone whom one really liked and for no reason other than what appeared to be a minor disagreement. But this difference in opinion was magnified into gross disloyalty, and the fellowship was shown to be merely a mechanism of mutual convenience. It is because so many marriages are based on a sincere, immature affection rather than love that they often fail to endure. This does not mean that affection is of no avail; it simply states that while affection provides a necessary atmosphere in which a relationship can flourish, if it is to grow into a durable, stable structure there must be a sure foundation of mutual love. Love alone can withstand the turmoil and the drudgery of unromantic daily life, because both partners are giving unsparingly of themselves for the common good even when they feel bored, depressed and generally disillusioned. Faith and hope bring a relationship to strength while love causes it to triumph over adversity.

The Decalogue is indeed still of paramount importance as the introduction to civilized living. It is the prerequisite for the spiritual life, indeed the essential foundation on which spirituality can develop. Until we are in right relationship with God and our neighbour, we will never be able to attain mystical illumination by means of specialized meditation techniques. There is in the world at present – and no doubt there always has been a similar tendency – a yearning for esoteric knowledge without reference to basic religious discipline. The hope is to transcend personal consciousness and enter the realms of the divine without adjusting one's life to the requirements of basic morality. True spirituality is based on the hard foundation of right action in the world; if the foundation is unstable the esoteric edifice will soon collapse. Thus the great religious traditions stand the test of time, whereas the cults have a mushroom growth and disappearance.

The Ten Commandments stress the fact that love is a discipline. This discipline is embraced in all the statutes of the Law, and as we follow the decrees of God, so our will is strengthened and we are able to work as mature, responsible people. Love, furthermore, if it is real extends to all people, not only to those for whom we have a special affinity. As Jesus tells us, we have to love our enemies and pray for those who persecute us. This injunction cannot be obeyed on the spur of the moment. It entails much heart-searching, much acquaintance with the dark side of oneself, much humility and constant honesty with courage before we can accept someone who is a perpetual source of antagonism and disharmony. We are not expected to exonerate or excuse that person any more than we are to castigate ourself for our lack of forbearance and charity. On the contrary, we have to see the truth clearly and with detachment, and then acknowledge God's gift of himself to us, joyfully proclaiming our own identity. In the state of blessed equanimity we can flow out in genuine acceptance to other people also; in so doing we become instruments of their healing by the grace of God that radiates from us. All this takes time and effort. We are confronted time after time by a sense of heartbreaking failure as the old Adam reasserts itself and demands recompense for what it has done.

In the same way a relationship has to be fostered; much labour has to be expended on it. At first we respond to the lovable qualities of the other person, but as the relationship deepens, so we are confronted by less agreeable traits, while at the same time the darkness in ourself is also brought to the surface. All these conflicting aspects of the personality have to be faced, accepted, loved and finally integrated into the relationship. When the work is pursued with courage and faith, the less attractive aspects of both personalities are gradually healed. Eventually there may occur a transfiguration of both people as they enter the life of mature responsibility that brings them to the divine relationship. It is the acceptance of darkness and its exposure to the light in the face of God that is the essential work of love, both in oneself and in the other person. This is a far cry from an attitude of goodwill or a feeling of affection such as we may evince on a special occasion of general rejoicing.

What have the Ten Commandments to say to our present condition? Are they not irrelevant in an age of such impermanence that no one can forecast the future even a few months ahead? Traditional moral values seem to be placed on one side by the threat of imminent annihilation such as nuclear warfare now poses. What can the younger generation say to a system of values based on a secure family unit and national integrity when many people may never find employment? Are we all, and especially the young, not justified in living life to the full now without reflecting on moral consequences, for who knows what tomorrow may bring in the wake of an international disaster? It must be said at once that there are no easy solutions to the worldwide economic recession and to the paucity of employment that has followed on it any more than there are to the nuclear arms-race. For the unemployment crisis to be positively approached there will have to be a new spirit of sacrifice and responsibility all round so that we can share what resources are available with loving accord. The threat of nuclear destruction can be averted only by a greater change in heart of all people, so that there is trust and co-operation between the super-powers where there is at present only fear and distrust. None of this can be organized; it has to spring from the heart made humble and now open to God's love. At present there is an atmosphere of material disillusionment and spiritual aspiration among many people living in the more developed countries, and one encouraging sign of inner renewal is a deepening awareness of personal responsibility in the world's troubles. No longer can injustice remain hidden under a cloak of ignorance, nor can the feelings of the individual remain stifled beneath the decorum of conventional religion.

In the past, maintenance of the *status quo* was the excuse for tolerating social abuses, whereas nowadays the establishment is generally the target for all destructive criticism. Unfortunately, those who rail at the traditional established order often have little to put in its place that would significantly improve the lot of the common man. The revolutionary establishments do not in the end seem to bring greater happiness than did their reactionary predecessors. The reason for this depends on the sad truth that while names and politics may change, the personal presence at the helm of government remains imperfect. It continues to be subject to the power of selfish abuse that we call sin. Social injustice breeds evil and should certainly be remedied at once. Nevertheless, it is unlikely that the worldly millennium itself would see the end of personal sin, for man does not live by bread alone. Certainly the very rich are often extremely unhappy in their personal lives. Man does not belong primarily to this world. It is his place of sojourn during the brief period of his incarnation, but his true self lives in an eternal realm and finds its home only in God. Therefore the divine presence has to inform all our earthly endeavours. Only then will they be lifted up from expediency to permanence, from belligerent gestures against a ruling class to works of reconciliation in which all people may be healed and sanctified.

The personal value of the Ten Commandments and their counterparts in the other world faiths is that they cause us to develop the will. To face the temptation to steal, even by slightly falsifying an income-tax return, and to conquer it, is a personal triumph. Likewise, to face lustful thoughts and then to put them behind one is an affirmation of the power of self-control over powerful impulses deep in the unconscious. It is similarly a moment of celebration when one can resist the temptation to join in an orgy of criticism of an absent colleague, when one can desist from idle gossip and mean scandal while one keeps one's own counsel. Indeed, the practice of silence is the first step in spiritual growth, so that when one does speak out it is for good purpose, such as exposing corruption or defending the weak and helpless against the cruelty of the strong and able-bodied. Then one's words carry weight, for they are considered and purposeful, not rash outbursts of abuse that are merely destructive if indeed they have any effect at all. Needless to say, none of this is possible on a long-term basis until we are in right relationship with God. In fact, the primary act of will is prayer. Therefore the first three commandments stand at the head of our spiritual life to guide us in the way of considered social action to our parents, those whom we meet day by day and the general run of mankind. Once our prayer life is in order, our will becomes strengthened and increasingly decisive, and our relationships honest and loving. The Decalogue and its various counterparts in the other great religions lead us to the fulfilled life.

Even if we lack employment, we can still behave in a civilized way. The very lack of organized work gives us more opportunity to bring peace and comfort to those around us. This is in fact a major function of the elderly, retired members of society. When we can no longer be active in the streets, we can still disport an active mind and share that activity in listening and giving counsel. One's past experience can act as a well-proven textbook. Furthermore, an attitude of patient concern is more likely to attract work to a younger person than one of idleness or general antagonism to society because of his unemployment. The work that ultimately matters is being of use to those around one at the present moment. If one gives of oneself in a small situation, a larger work will become available as one shows oneself ready to receive it. The person who obeys the moral law will tend to be more attractive to a potential employer than one whose life is undisciplined. What we are radiates from our presence, and those with discernment will soon select the best applicant.

In the realm of sexual relationships there has been the greatest revolution of all, and this within the last few decades. Nowadays honesty of feeling is the essential criterion, and to many observers any type of intercourse between consenting adults is regarded as acceptable. The equation of sin and sexual intercourse outside marriage is now, at least for the great majority of people, a thing of the past. It may well be effectively argued that a probationary period of cohabitation should precede all marriages, in order to cut down the high divorce rate. But it has to be added that living together in an affectionate *ménage* is a long way from marriage. The difference between affection and love is seen very clearly in this contrasted situation. A premeditated living together, however affectionate, can be terminated at any time, whereas love is indissoluble. As St Paul puts it, 'There is nothing love cannot face; there is no limit to its faith, its hope and its endurance. Love will never come to an end' (1 Corinthians 13.7–8). Commitment is at the heart of love, and it flows out to the offspring as well as to the other partner. The offspring of unmarried couples lack a basic security that is the fruit of the marital status. On the other hand, marriage should not be undertaken until there is a sober commitment to honour one's pledges to the end of life. This commitment brings with it a searing self-knowledge and a deep emotional link with one's partner. The stress laid on an inviolate family life has been instrumental in the survival of the Jews as an influential group in the world up to this day; their great contribution in the realm of the mind and spirit at least equals their material competence, and that despite the terrible persecutions to which they have been subjected over the centuries. Admittedly the concept of the family has to be widened to embrace all people, but it starts with those close to us in blood and marriage relationships. Once it has been proved on this circumscribed level, it is worthy of extension outwards to include other people in its range.

In the same way, charity does begin at home, but it should not end there. When love reigns in our hearts, it radiates spontaneously from us to our neighbour and outwards to the whole world in passionate intercessory prayer. Commitment leads to spiritual growth, whereas selfish indulgence tends towards stagnation. This is perhaps the essential difference in effect between an affectionate cohabitation and a marriage. There is a point in honouring our parents provided they have proved themselves worthy of honour. There is a difference between married parents and an affectionate couple who live together for a time, bear children and then separate. The end will be a one-parent family, and the parent who has defected can hardly deserve any honour at all. The slipshod bringing up of children bears its own reward in later delinquency. Where there has been no love, the child lacks emotional roots and is all too liable to drift into any unpleasant association.

It needs finally to be said that love does not evade truth. If a person has behaved badly or is offensive to other people, he must be confronted with his actions and the effects they are producing on those around him. To permit him to continue in a socially unacceptable way lest he resents adverse criticism is a mark of cowardice, not love. The dictum of Proverbs 13.24, already quoted, is worth constant reflection: a father who spares the rod hates his son, but one who loves him keeps him in order. Jesus' equally cogent injunctions about loving our enemies and praying for our persecutors does not annul this dictum; rather, it gives it point and purpose. If we react directly and promptly to injustice or socially unacceptable behaviour, we set the wrongdoer on the right course, and as long as he fails to respond, he cuts himself off from the company of his peers. Indeed, a period in the wilderness is an important experience for getting us to know ourself better in complete silence: we return chastened, wiser and more capable of playing our part constructively in our social milieu. Jesus' equally severe injunction against judging other people does not forbid us to evaluate actions. He himself warns us to beware of false prophets, whom we will recognize by the fruits they bear (Matthew 7.15–16). The fruits of our actions have always to be carefully assessed. The wrongdoer, by contrast, should not be judged so much as understood. We do not know the circumstances that have led him into an unacceptable way of life; usually it is a combination of social deprivation and personal inadequacy. Christ could heal the personal factor so that the offender could cope more effectively with the social side. Nowadays we strive, quite rightly, to set the environment in good order as far as possible, but our success in dealing with personal weaknesses is limited. Jeremiah's rhetorical question, 'Can the Nubian change his skin, or the leopard his spots?' (Jeremiah 13.23), applies all too well to ourself in our personal problems. Only a love such as that of Christ, can produce an inner transformation. Judgement, by contrast, simply confirms the defect, but does nothing to heal it.

Jesus said, 'Do not suppose that I have come to abolish the Law and the prophets; I did not come to abolish, but to complete. I tell you this: so long as heaven and earth endure, not a letter, not a stroke, will disappear from the Law until all that must happen has happened' (Matthew 5.17–18). Obedience to the Law develops the power of the will, but what Christ brought was the spirit of love. With it the demands of the Law could be fulfilled effortlessly in response to God's call upon us, and universally among all people. In Christ the will of God and man coincide; neither is weakened or deflected. On the contrary, the human will is transfigured to a burning concern for the welfare of all creatures. When all that the Law stands for is achieved, it will have served its purpose. Then it will be inscribed on the heart and become the unwritten law of heavenly love.

So prophesied Jeremiah about 600 years before Christ:

This is the covenant which I shall make with Israel after those days, says the Lord; I will set my law within them and write it on their hearts; I will become their God and they shall be my people. No longer need they teach one another to know the Lord; all of them, high and low alike, shall know me, says the Lord, for I will forgive their wrongdoing and remember their sin no more (Jeremiah 31.33–4).

What was shown to Jeremiah was fulfilled by Jesus on the cross when he bore the collective sin of the world and poured out forgiveness on those who could not understand. At that moment love entered fully into the world. But until we can accept that love and give it without restraint to all those around us, the Law must remain both our guide to the moral life and our condemnation when we fall on the way. Nevertheless, God stands close behind us in our failures and follies. We must hope that when we have almost succumbed to the madness of nuclear warfare, he will emerge and awaken us to our full estate, which is eternity. At present mankind seems asleep and in the throes of troubled dreams. But when we awake we will find ourselves at the end of the path, and Christ will be there to receive us in the name of the Father and the power of the Holy Spirit. At last we will emerge integrated people in the image of Christ himself. In him the Law and the prophets are fulfilled; they are transfigured into a beacon of uncreated light such as attended Jesus at the time of his own transfiguration. That light will bathe the world in divine radiance prior to its resurrection.